School Reform in the Deep South

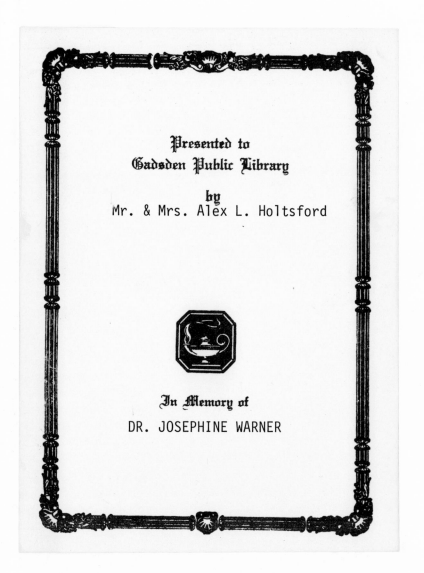

School Reform
in the
Deep South

A Critical Appraisal

Edited by

DAVID J. VOLD *&* JOSEPH L. DeVITIS

THE UNIVERSITY OF ALABAMA PRESS
TUSCALOOSA AND LONDON

The paper on which this book is printed meets the minimum re-
quirements of American National Standard for Information
Science-Permanence of Paper for Printed Library Materials,
ANSI A39.48-1984.

Library of Congress Cataloging-in-Publication Data

School reform in the Deep South : a critical appraisal / edited by
  David J. Vold and Joseph L. DeVitis.
    p.   cm.
  Includes bibliographical references and index.
  ISBN 0-8173-0553-X
    1. Public schools—Southern States.   2. Educational change—
Southern States.   3. Educational change—Alabama.   I. Vold,
David J., 1947–   . II. DeVitis, Joseph L.
LA230.5.S6S36   1991   90–44661
370'.975—dc20   ABL-5558

British Library Cataloguing-in-Publication Data available

"Public Education's Last Hurrah? Schizophrenia, Amnesia, and Ignorance in
School Politics," by William Lowe Boyd, was first published in *Educational
Evaluation and Policy Analysis,* Vol. 9, no. 2, pp. 85–110. It is published here,
as edited, by permission of the author and the American Educational Research
Association. The volume editors are grateful to the College of Education at The
University of Alabama for paying for permission to republish this chapter.

"The Illusion of Educational Reform in Georgia," by Wayne J. Urban, was first
published in *Journal of Thought,* Vol. 22, no. 2, pp. 31–36. It is published here,
as edited, by permission of the author and the editor of *Journal of Thought.*

"Democratic Tension and the Future of the Public School," by David J. Vold,
was first published as "Private Rights Versus Public Welfare" Democratic Tension and the Public School," in *Toward Tomorrow,* pp. 38–45, the 1983 proceedings of the Southern World Future Society. It is published here, as edited and
retitled, by permission of the author and the editor of the proceedings.

Contents

Part Three

Introduction

DAVID J. VOLD & JOSEPH L. DeVITIS

I cannot in any degree approve of those restless and busy med-dlers who, called by neither birth nor fortune to take part in the management of public affairs, are yet always projecting reforms; and if I thought that this track contained aught which might justify the suspicion that I was victim of such folly, I would by no means permit its publication. I have never contemplated any-thing higher than the reformation of my own opinions, and bas-ing them on a foundation wholly my own.

—*Descartes*

Reform movements come and go. In their heyday, they look as if they might sweep away all the cobwebs of stagnation and recalcitrance to which institutions and societies are subject. But after only a few years, the reform that once looked so prom-ising often lies forgotten, only to be replaced by yet another "sure-fire" reform. What is the legacy of reform? Why aren't we more successful in our reform efforts?

In retrospect, reform proposals sometimes appear to have been quite foolish—even those that may have garnered a substantial following for a time. Nevertheless, much can be learned by reflecting on our attempts at reform—foolish or not. Reflection is not just a way of burying a dead reform; it enables us to squeeze some life out of what otherwise would have been just another failed program. The opportunity exists for genuine improvement, but it is missed whether we go complacently along with new policies or we just bide our time, waiting for the reform movement to pass.

School reform in the Southeast offers especially promising grist for the mill of critical appraisal. In the first place, few areas of the country have endured the educational ignominy of the Southeast, and the national mood of reform has caught a strong current of support there. That support stems primarily from the popular assumption that a region's economic achievement is determined by its educational achievement, but it is also a function of southern discomfort with the role of perennial underachiever. If a national mood of dissatisfaction with public schooling exists (i.e., if the iron is hot), then many southern boosters have concluded that this may be the best time to strike. There may be no better time than the present to make southern schools as good as—or better than—those found in other parts of the country. A sense of urgency attached to school reform makes it dangerous; in the rush to get results, poor solutions often win powerful support.

Once a school reform proposal is adopted, one of four outcomes will occur: (1) nothing at all might happen (i.e., the school program may continue with no discernible difference), (2) the schools might get better, (3) the schools might get worse, or (4) the schools might be abandoned altogether (i.e., the public might get out of the school business, leaving it to private enterprise). While the South may be as susceptible to the second and third alternatives as the rest of the country, it is probably more susceptible to the first and fourth alternatives.

Since colonial times, laissez-faire thinking—politically and economically—has held greater sway in the South than in the rest of the country. It was this laissez-faire predisposition that led the South, in the nineteenth century, to view national politics as a threat and to secede from the Union. In the twentieth century, it led Governor George Wallace, in the name of states' rights, to stand up to the federal government and attempt to block the way of a black student who sought to register at The University of Alabama. It made the South slower to accept public schooling or to implement compulsory schooling. It is what made the elimination of compulsory education possible in Mississippi, following the *Brown* decision of 1954. It made the establishment of segregation academies thinkable in innumerable southern communities; it stems not from racism per se but from the widespread acceptance of schooling as an individual matter—not a social concern. While that view finds expression everywhere, its roots run deeper in the South. It is laissez-faire thinking that keeps southern property taxes low and the public schools underfunded.

This laissez-faire attitude is captured exactly in the following letter to the editor of a southern newspaper regarding the defeat of a property tax proposal.

> Congratulations to county voters for their rejection to the property tax increase. Personally, I am not against increased funding for the county school system. No doubt, additional funding may be needed. What I am hopeful the county voters were saying is they are opposed to the method of increased funding. That is my only objection to property tax increases for education.
>
> Contrary to popular belief, there are fair taxes. However, this was not one. This would unfairly tax some people without school children, while some who do have school children are paying little or no property tax. Is it equitable for the ones not using the system to pay for those who are using the system and yet not paying for the system?
>
> If those who use the county schools want to raise money, would it be fair for them to force others (who do not use the school) to pay for education just because they want increased funding? To my knowledge, there is no law that prohibits donations to the schools. Well then, let the people who think the schools need funding donate all they please.
>
> The problem is not one of irresponsibility on the part of county voters, but one of responsibility on the parents who have children in school. If the parents want their children in school, then let these parents pay for this education. Do not send the bill around the corner to your neighbor.
>
> What is an example of fair taxation? A toll road is one. Only people who use it pay.[1]

Where reform efforts will lead, how far reform will go, whether there will be any reform—in the South, in particular—are questions that will be addressed in the context of laissez-faire thinking.

Still, these are heady times. A feeling exists that something momentous is in the air. We seem to be at a historical watershed, a window of opportunity. If we drag our feet, the opportunity may be lost. On the other hand, if our decisions are foolish, the opportunity is likely to turn into catastrophe. Already, we see evidence that educators and politicians who were quick to join the reform movement may be looking for ways to bail out. Of course, reform costs money, but more disturbing than that is the real fear that increased spending won't bring improved quality. While "reform" is always popular, proposed reform measures often face enormous opposition: this opposition often originates within educational organizations, but eventually it spills over to the public. What is most evident is that considerable disagreement exists over just what constitutes reform.

It is obvious that reform entails change, but what kind of change? It is not enough to say that it is change for the better—that is as obvious as it is useless. How do we distinguish between appearance and reality? How can we know what is better?

While "reform" is clearly "change for the better," the two terms are not entirely interchangeable. We note, for instance, that "reform" is never attached to commercial products—soaps are advertised as "new" and "improved," never as "reformed." On the other hand, criminals who have turned over a new leaf are usually described as "reformed" (and never "improved," although "improved" is applied to the criminal's behavior). Juvenile delinquents might be sent to a reform school, but not to take courses in self-improvement. But if reform seems to be distinctively linked to people as opposed to material things, it also applies to institutions (organizations of people). Significant changes in the church, the school, and in government are often called reforms.

One classic model of reform is *the* Reformation. The object of the Protestant Reformation was to restore the Church to a lost state of righteousness, the key being "to restore." As such, the reformers saw themselves as conservative agents even though their actions were revolutionary. Not all reforms aim at restoration, of course.

R*eform* implies r*eorganization.* That may entail reconstruction—progress toward a determined, or even an undetermined, end. What is required is that the present situation be viewed as essentially flawed. The first step is to identify and defeat what is wrong and then replace it with what is right. This is why, in part, soap is sold not as "reformed" but as "improved." If our reform efforts are to be successful, we must engage in the philosophical task of answering such questions as: "What do we want?" "What are we trying to accomplish?" "What ought education to be about anyway?" But, we must also ask, "What are our schools doing wrong?"

We reform our schools because we believe that they are not really educating our children, and we believe that reform will lead to better education. We might even regard what is being done in the name of education actually to be miseducative. But therein lies the rub. We do not all agree about the meaning of education, let alone "better" education. That realization ought to motivate us to ask why. Even more disturbing than our lack of consensus regarding the meaning of education is the fact that few people seem disturbed by it. What gets our attention is falling test scores, and whatever leads to an improvement in test scores is assumed to constitute reform. But "majority opinion"—and intellectual complacency—both do not preclude the possibility of our stepping over a historical precipice.

We are the fortunate heirs of a democratic tradition. Yet, that tradition is perverted by an opinion poll mentality that encourages decision making by raising a wet finger in the wind. We seem to assume that all that is required to move ahead is 50 percent plus one. But voting is less crucial to the preservation of a healthy democracy than deliberation and shared participation.

Alas, the bandwagons that command so much attention seldom slow down for people to reflect on the directions in which they are heading. Even educators who are professionally responsible for the conduct of schooling too seldom provide the kind of interpretation that the public ought to have to choose intelligently. We educators too frequently lead the parade.[2]

Indeed, during the past several years, the American public has been inundated by a plethora of education reform reports both outside and within the world of professional education, beginning with *A Nation at Risk* (National Commission on Excellence in Education, 1983), through *A Call for Change in Teacher Education* (American Association of Colleges for Teacher Education, 1985), to more recent reports of the Holmes Group consortium of education deans (1986), the Carnegie Commission on Education and the Economy (1986), "A World of Differences" (Educational Testing Service, 1989), and "Everybody Counts: A Report to the Nation on the Future of Mathematics Education" (National Research Council, 1989). All these reports represent powerful constituencies at the national level. At the same time, a majority of state legislatures, boards, and departments of education, usually cajoled by state governors (especially, but not exclusively, in the Southeast), have begun to mandate increased credentialing and testing of teachers.

With respect to many of these recent national commission reports on education, most notably *A Nation at Risk,* some commentators (though not the majority of the popular press) have perceptively identified underlying political intentions and effects in the reports themselves.

> [These reports] do have their function in American politics, but fact-finding, rigorous analysis, and policy development are usually not among them. Commissions are appropriate for dramatizing an issue, resolving political differences, and reassuring the public that questions are being thoughtfully considered.[3]

> [Yet] the contemporary discourse denies complexity in our institutions by relying upon ahistorical, asocial reasoning. As political documents, the reforms pursue the wrong strategies for the right purposes, posing contradictions. As intellectual documents, folklore is accepted instead of scholarship.[4]

Such reform measures are endemic of a wider pernicious tendency in the history of American education. Whenever given publics do not seem to want to face broader social problems in serious, head-on fashion, they tend to blame the schools for a significant measure of their own public neglect or malfeasance. In its relatively brief history, public education has been cited (akin to Dr. Smith's or Father John's elixir) as either the cause or cure for most of America's organic ills, for example, poverty, crime, vice, low industrial productivity and quality control, and even for the decline in American prestige across the world. This is particularly the case if one were to believe such critics as Hyman Rickover, James B. Conant, Terrel H. Bell, Chester Finn, and William Bennett.

Ironically, while the totality of American educational history suggests that our publics cherish diversity in school policy and practices, the current state reform movements increase the likelihood of nationalization and homogenization of school policy. Historical reality could be dramatically transformed in the present decade.

In the broad sweep of contemporary history, school reform has been marked by cyclical tides that seem to ebb and flow toward either "academic content" orientations (in the 1950s and mid-1970s to the present) or concern for social and psychological issues (in the 1960s and early 1970s).[5] Such circumstances provide some educators uneasy pause for consideration: Which school reform will be in vogue next year? Yet, an important missing element would appear to underlie any lasting, meaningful opportunity for significant change: simultaneous, synergistic efforts aimed at systemic restructuring at all societal levels. A. Harry Passow poses this case in stark terms: "All of us have a role to play in reforming our schools and our society. Reforming schools, however, is very different from reforming society. . . . Both must occur simultaneously if real reform is to take place."[6]

If Passow is correct, there is considerable reason for pessimism, as criticism of the current reform movement has noted that

> Despite their religious-revivalist tone and calls for reform, the [reform] reports are essentially conservative documents that reflect a narrow *technocratic rationality*—a mode of reasoning, in-

vestigation, or planning that gives priority to considerations of procedure or technique. Questions of purpose and substance, of value and interest, tend to be ignored. . . . The reports do not significantly challenge the status quo within or outside school curriculum. . . . Purposes are taken for granted, and focus is given to means of accomplishing presumably consensually defined goals. In the name of excellence, the emphasis is on standardization . . . , not reform.[7]

Still, the Carnegie Task Force on Teaching as a Profession (1986) proposed that some forty billion dollars be spent to harness structural redesigns throughout educational and societal institutions. Such a recommendation poses a painful test of commitment for a citizenry and political leadership in the throes of an ever-lengthening "me-decade" characterized by a kind of "meanness mania" toward larger social programs and social consciousness in general.[8] Ironically, two states that purport to be leaders in the school reform movement in the Southeast (viz., Tennessee and Florida) have been providing less fiscal support for education than they did before "reform" began in the early 1980s. In 1985–86, the state of Tennessee actually spent more public funds on the evaluation of teachers than it did for total merit pay for all the teachers in Tennessee who so qualified. In 1986–87, starting teacher salaries in Tennessee were at the bottom of the Southeast and the nation despite the public-relations glitter and rhetoric of its "Better Schools" program. In light of such circumstances, one need not wonder why the school reform movement has tended to demoralize the teaching profession.[9]

Meanwhile, the 1986 Carnegie report also called both for higher teacher status and for vastly increased salaries that will allow teachers to compete with other professionals both at the entry level and at advanced career stages. As a practical matter, to do otherwise might well contribute to teacher shortage in the very near future like that of the 1950s and 1960s.[10] For example, in Tennessee alone it is estimated that some 25,000 new teachers will be needed by 1993. Though some southeastern states have increased teacher salaries, the general scale for the region still falls markedly behind those in other regions. With "stop-gap" recruits called into the profession (often people unable to find another job), real matters of "quality" and "excellence" would seem to be further neglected. This quandary should prompt a serious pause for some governors in the Southeast, as well as for the Southern Regional Education Board, who have encouraged "alternative routes" to teacher certification for candidates without fully articulated, professional degree programs in education.

Teachers in the trenches should not be expected to be too patient with public posturing among politicians, policymakers, government officials, and educational leaders who play parlor games with one of the most precious of human activities. If teachers cannot fully control their wider social, political, and economic destinies, they still possess substantial responsibility for participating in "tough" and "tender" dialogue on the important questions facing their own profession today. Teachers want to be accountable for policies and practices that they themselves have had a hand in creating. Teachers should not be counted on to countenance a "top-down" approach to reform, as has been the case in the recent past, and still be expected to be ready, willing, and able to "perform as told." Teachers do not see themselves as hired hands but as participant-creators in their professional enterprise; and education will never become a true, or fully humane, profession so long as they are treated in a less than completely collaborative fashion.

The essays in this volume speak to many of the above concerns in timely, sometimes piercing, and often eloquent manner. They are not intended to proffer any "quick-fix" solutions or ultimate panaceas; such attempts may have already tended to exacerbate existing problems. Indeed, any ill-conceived, precipitate rush for "reform," without careful consideration of likely and potential consequences, would seem to be fraught with possibilities for unintended mistakes and adverse outcomes. Unfortunately, we have already witnessed some of the latter. Nor is this book meant to fuel the fire of political posturing, though we do hope that it will contribute to public discourse on a wide range of reform issues. Instead, its fundamental purpose is to appraise—in interpretive, normative, and critical ways—the school reform movement in general. Although the focus is on the Southeast, we do not intend a state-by-state survey; our concern is philosophical rather than descriptive. A few states—in particular the Deep South states of Mississippi, Alabama, and Georgia (states that are often overlooked in the educational reform literature)—will be examined in detail as will some of the more significant issues that surround reform efforts. Our overall aim is to raise the questions that might salvage some possibility of improvement from what have been essentially failed reform programs. It is our goal that these questions may be used by diverse groups and participants both inside and outside the schools to start on new paths to education.

If we are to bring about reform in our schools, we must restore a true sense of education to them. This does not mean that we should make them more like they were in the 1960s or the 1950s or even the 1890s. If the truth be known, we have never educated students as well as we might. Yet, if education has not flourished, it has survived. If we are to strengthen it, we must know what it is that we are strengthening. Too often, reformers are asking the wrong questions or, worse, no questions at all. If we will begin to argue about what an education might mean rather than how to raise test scores, the reform of American education will be pointed in the right direction. If we will couple argument with tolerance of diversity in ideas, our progress will be assured.

This book is divided into three parts. The first part establishes the framework for educational reform and explores some of the major issues that have emerged. The second part takes up the specifics of reform programs, focusing on the three Deep South states of Mississippi, Alabama, and Georgia. Finally, Part Three reflects on what may come if we fail in our reform efforts.

The first step is taken in the opening chapter, "Public Education's Last Hurrah? Schizophrenia, Amnesia, and Ignorance in School Politics." It is written by William Lowe Boyd, a professor of education at Pennsylvania State University and an expert on school policy and politics and educational administration. While not strictly focused on the Southeast, this chapter helps to set the stage for the chapters that follow. Boyd examines the reform movement from a sociological perspective, explores its weaknesses, and proposes a realistic approach. His primary concern is that we seize the current opportunity to reform the public schools without jeopardizing their existence, an opportunity we will miss if we continue to employ a top-down—especially a "bully pulpit"—approach to reform.

The top-down approach to educational reform is the subject of "Bill Clinton and Arkansas: Can Political Leaders Reform the Schools?" The author is Robert W. Johns, a professor of social studies education and curriculum and instruction at the University of Arkansas at Little Rock. Johns reflects on the role the governor of Arkansas has played in that state's reform efforts. Although he finds little in Arkansas's reform experience that gives rise to optimism, he directs our attention to one seldom advocated but promising possibility, namely, the small-school concept.

In his chapter, C. J. B. Macmillan, a professor of philosophy of education at Florida State University, introduces us to yet another reform issue, "Curriculum Reform and Professional Expertise: The Florida Experience." Macmillan alerts us to the conflict implicit in the two worthy reform goals of (1) "providing 'quality' academic education" and (2) "'expressing a higher regard for teachers.'" Macmillan argues that school reform tends to undermine teacher professionalism by reflecting a distrust of the teacher's ability. Ultimately, we will have to decide whether to allow teachers autonomy. Macmillan contends that, in the long run, the professional growth of teachers will benefit the students more than all of our reform proposals that are designed to protect the system from the effects of incompetent teachers.

Just as some reform proposals have been aimed at making the schools "teacher-proof" (i.e., immune to the effects of incompetent teachers), others attempt to reward the best and attract excellent prospects into the teacher ranks. Perhaps the most controversial of the many reform proposals is merit pay.

In the last chapter of Part One, Kenneth D. McCracken, a

professor of curriculum and instruction at the University of Tennessee at Martin, and David J. Vold, professor of history and philosophy of education at The University of Alabama, examine the merit-pay proposal. While not ruling out merit pay out of hand, they argue against simplistic understandings of merit. They conclude that merit pay can only be successful when teachers have a clear hand in developing the criteria for measuring it, when it is used to enhance the professional stature of teachers beyond their school districts, when it is accompanied by a substantial base-pay increase, and when it is tied to earned university degrees emphasizing theoretical grounding in education.

Up to this point, our focus has been on particular reform *issues.* Now we shift our attention to particular reform *movements,* beginning with Mississippi.

The opening of Part Two takes up the question of educational reform in Mississippi, especially the Mississippi Education Reform Act of 1982. The authors, William A. Person, a professor of curriculum and instruction, and Robert L. Jenkins, a professor of history—both at Mississippi State University—report that many of the reforms introduced in 1982 were anything but new. Yet, despite clear and positive rhetoric in support of the public schools, the record indicates a consistent failure to fund them adequately.

"Educational Reform in Alabama: 1972–1989," is the subject of the next chapter. Charles F. Rudder, a professor of history and philosophy of education at The University of Alabama, begins with a detailed summary and analysis of the developments in educational policy and practice in that state during the last two decades. He concludes that, while much has changed over this period, few of the changes have been directed toward reform. Perhaps more disturbing than that, Rudder describes what reform there has been as largely irrational.

Yet, "our dismal record" of school reform should not lead us to conclude that nothing can be done. Rather, it ought to prompt us to reconceive the problem. Rudder argues that the problem of education (and, hence, educational reform) needs to be recast—from a mechanical-linear model to an organic one.

The gist of his argument is for the primacy of theory in educational decision making and for consistency between policy and practice by educational leaders.

While Rudder argues for greater attention to educational theory, Wayne J. Urban contends, in his chapter, that many who have a stake in education are pointedly left out of the discussion. Urban, a professor of history of education at Georgia State University, shows that the educational reform movement is dominated by "a powerful coalition of established individuals and groups seeking to force their will on our schools, their teachers, and students." Because of this situation, even though educational reform efforts in Georgia are "overrated in significance," what does occur is "pernicious in its effects."

Having considered several important reform issues and the efforts at reform in Mississippi, Alabama, and Georgia, we take up in Part Three a very different agenda but one that is introduced in the opening of Part One. There, Boyd notes that "support for public schools is endangered by fundamental demographic and value shifts" and that "current reform efforts could turn out to be public education's 'last hurrah.'" Part Three presents reflections on this possibility, namely, the deregulation of schooling.

Deregulation is a theme that began to emerge in the 1970s, but it had little significant support until the overwhelming chorus of public school criticism reached its zenith in the 1980s. This development has apparently produced the common wisdom that the public schools are a failed institution. Some would argue that the failure is inherent, stemming from government involvement. That is the perspective found in the next chapter.

"Imagining Sisyphus Happy with Educational Reformers," written by David E. Denton, a professor of philosophy of education at the University of Kentucky, stands in sharp contrast with the preceding chapters, but only in the sense that he appears willing to abandon public schooling. Denton examines the meaning of "reform" and explores the possibilities of the educational reform movement. Rejecting "methodism" on the one hand and "fundamentalism" on the other, he argues for a third alternative, "the ontological one," by which he means being open to images of possibilities regarding what it might mean to be an adult and regarding what our culture can become. If we are to be open to individual and cultural possibility, Denton concludes we must allow individuals and communities (as opposed to the state) the greatest possible freedom in pursuing their own future—in pursuing their own education. In short, he argues that real reform awaits the abolition of government schooling.

This "solution" has much to recommend it. It appears to provide much more freedom to the individual; it also puts the power of competition and private enterprise into the mix. There are those who claim we can already get a glimpse of what deregulation would mean: many private schools are touted as having an entire student body with scores at or above the 90th percentile on standardized tests (the high scores are attributed to the influence of the private school in question, although the connection is not demonstrated). Of course, this kind of comparison (private schools at the 90th percentile, public schools at the 50th percentile) is spurious—public schools are much more broadly representative than private schools—yet invidious comparisons continue to be made and outrageous claims continue to be voiced.

In all fairness, it should be noted that Denton does not make his appeal for educational vouchers based on such comparisons. Denton believes in the absolute value of freedom and that vouchers would provide individuals with the greatest amount of freedom in determining their own education. Thus, he regards vouchers as the moral alternative to the essentially immoral "group mind" supposedly engendered by public schooling. That reform efforts also appear to have been futile is fuel to add to his fire.

In the concluding chapter, on the other hand, David J. Vold argues that vouchers (or tuition tax credits, i.e., policies that would lead to the privatization of American schooling) would not produce reform. While most advocates of deregulation argue from the premise of individualism, the litmus test of any policy is the health of society. Vold argues that the preponderance of evidence for a healthy society is on the side of public schooling. Yet, the priority of society need not mean that the individual is overlooked. What is required is that the public school districts be sufficiently small for the individual to have a meaningful role in their governance. This structure would not solve all the problems the schools face, but it does give them a democratic means for addressing them. Ultimately, it is in the democratic social theater that the problem of education will be "solved" and "resolved."

In these pages, we are attempting to review some reform proposals and their consequences. We see that reforms, which are introduced with great fanfare and promise, often crumble under scrutiny. Would-be reform seldom seems to move beyond the would-be. If this situation is discouraging it should also serve to remind us of the importance of education and caution us against abandoning the struggle to attain it. It should also remind us of the need to keep our focus on educational theory and let that be our guide and not to allow reaction to dictate our policies. Finally, we should bear in mind that times of criticism are times of promise and opportunity. What are the opportunities that await us?

Part One

Public Education's Last Hurrah? Schizophrenia, Amnesia, and Ignorance in School Politics

WILLIAM LOWE BOYD

Like *A Nation at Risk*, most of the wave of national reports and policy discussion that came on its heels is marred by elements of schizophrenia, amnesia, and ignorance about educational politics. As a consequence, the frequently misguided "top-down" reform strategies that have been prompted may backfire. Already we see signs that this is happening. If such a trend develops widely, further disillusionment with public schools and a consequent increase in support for privatization of schooling could occur. Rather than bringing a renaissance for public schools, current reform efforts could turn out to be public education's "last hurrah."

These bleak thoughts go against the grain of the optimism the statewide excellence movement has generated. But if they are valid, they clearly have serious implications for current reform policies and the future of public schooling in the United States. In brief, the argument presented here is, first, that success in the present reform movement is critical because support for public schools is endangered by fundamental demographic and value shifts; second, that reformers have been handicapped by an incomplete and inaccurate understanding of the politics and organizational character of schools; and, third, that their reform strategies consequently are often incongruent with the realities of changing schools. The purpose of this chapter is to examine the evidence on these propositions and then, in light of a keener sense of the social context of reform, to see what conclusions emerge about the most promising strategies for re-invigorating public schools.

Current Dangers

Could public education in the United States really be jeopardized by a failure of contemporary reform efforts? Some would say no real danger exists, that even if current reform efforts prove disappointing most Americans are firmly committed to support of public schools and won't be deterred by mediocre results from present efforts. After all, we've been reforming the public schools with modest results for generations and the public has remained loyal all along. Why should the present situation be any more precarious than the past?

What is new today are the serious implications of current social and demographic trends in the United States. Taken together, these trends indicate that public schools will find it increasingly difficult to retain broad-based public support. To begin with, there is the growth in the proportion of senior citizens in the population and the decline in the proportion of families with children in the public schools. Added to this trend is evidence that strongly suggests that public schools may have trouble retaining the support of middle and upper-middle class parents. One factor at work here is the increasing level of education in the populace generally and among the middle and upper-middle class in particular. As the educational level of families rise they tend to become more sophisticated, discerning, and demanding consumers of educational services. Schools are thus under pressure in part because of their very successes. Each generation tends to demand more from the schools than their predecessors. Thus the public, and especially the very highly educated upper-middle class, is increasingly quality conscious and unwilling to accept mediocre schooling services. As Fred M. Wirt has observed, education expands "their perspective on the possible, and they challenge what has been in order to fulfill their manifest capacities. As one political result, they question traditional values in every institution, evaluate the very utility of institutions themselves . . . and, in short, seek new policy directions."[1]

Another far-reaching development is that the public school population, particularly in urban areas, is composed increasingly of racial, ethnic, and language minority groups. These groups tend to have low political activity and influence and a high incidence of physical disabilities. As minority groups increasingly characterize the population of public schools, majority groups may become less willing to send their children to them and, consequently, to finance them. This pattern has been painfully clear for some time in many of our large city school systems. But added to this problem now is accumulating evidence that the affluent segment of the baby-boom generation is less committed to the support of the public schools than were their counterparts in earlier generations.[2]

A number of analysts argue that the maturation of the baby-boom generation has much to do with the dramatic reconfiguration of American politics since 1970. They stress that, unlike earlier generations influenced by the Great Depression and federal interventions to combat it, the "boomers" grew up with affluence and a sense that big government causes problems. With their basic materialistic needs satisfied, boomers seek self-actualization and inner directedness. According to Lee Atwater, one way this attitude manifests itself is with a concern for quality: "Bigger is not better anymore—better is better."[3] Consequently, boomers desire excellence and choice in schooling and may be skeptical of the ability of bureaucratized, government schools to deliver these qualities. Moreover, affluent boomers or "yuppies" (i.e., young urban professionals) generally can pay to get what they want because they often are double-wage-earner families with few children. As a result, they contribute significantly to the growing constituency in favor of excellence, choice, and privatization in education. A curb on this trend that should be noted, however, is the fact that a substantial portion of the boomer population is not only not affluent but actually facing a decline in their standard of living.

Assessing all of these trends and more, Paul E. Peterson concludes that the adaptive qualities and vast inertia of public schools as well-established institutions should carry them through these difficult times.[4] He notes also that private school costs and fees are likely to soar, pricing out many families and removing the threat of a large shift of enrollment from the public sector. Research on the Australian experience with private schools leads me to be more concerned about the vulnerability of public schools to private school competition. The experience "down under" shows clearly that you don't have to have a large private school enrollment (ours is now about 11 percent) to create and maintain a dual school system, with all of the associated problems of elitist private schools and demoralized government schools. What is critical is *who* goes to private schools. In Australia, 75 percent of the students still go to government schools. But the prestige and career advantages of attending the elite private schools (which charge substantial fees despite receiving state aid) foster a "creaming off" process that drains government high schools of most of their upper-middle class students. With the exodus of these students, the academic ethos and reputation of most government high schools decline sharply. Once set in motion this creaming off dynamic creates a vicious circle that ensures its own maintenance.

Significantly, a major conclusion of Peterson's own important historical research is that the strength of American public schools over time has depended on the support of the middle class and an ability to stave off competing institutions.[5] Yet, as Peterson recognizes, the public schools today face increasing competition, not only from private schools but also from day care and vocational training institutions. Indeed, the public schools now may be facing a more challenging environment than those to which they have responded successfully in the past. There can be little doubt about the enormous inertia of public schools, but their adaptive qualities might not be equal to the extraordinarily turbulent field they face due to a threatening combination of environmental trends over which they have no control.[6]

One possible scenario might run as follows: Because of mounting national concern about the need to promote U.S. economic competitiveness—coupled with revelations such as the continuing poor math performance of American students as compared to students from other nations—the view will continue to grow that improved educational achievement is imperative for better economic performance in this technological age. Suppose, then, that the "excellence" movement falters, public school performance lags, and there is growing acceptance of research claiming to document the inefficiency of public schools as compared to private schools. If these things happen, we then could witness the political sea change necessary for the creation of a new balance between public and private schools.

In sum, one does not have to be an alarmist to see that many current trends may sorely tax the adaptiveness and resilience of public schools. In view of the combination of factors eroding public support of public schools, we could face a real danger of public schools falling into a downward spiral of decay and disillusionment if the present reform movement stumbles. This is what Albert Shanker stresses when he speaks of the schools facing their "first real crisis."[7] The sociopolitical climate already has been receptive to the remarkable shift that the Reagan administration achieved in the overarching values guiding American educational policy. As D. L. Clark and T. A. Astuto demonstrate, through a systematic program of policies and pronouncements there has been a 180-degree shift in emphasis away from the values that guided federal policy in the 1970s: from equity to excellence; from needs and access to ability and selectivity; from regulations and enforcement to deregulation; from the common school to parental choice and institutional competition; and from social and welfare concerns to economic and productivity concerns.[8] Clearly, this shift in values challenges many of the traditional tenets of public education. It is in this context that we need to assess the status and use of knowledge about American educational politics in the contemporary school reform movement.

Schizophrenia in School Politics

Even a casual inspection of the literature on educational politics shows that much of it is schizophrenic. On one hand, it is argued that local control of schools and local influences on education have been reduced to no more than a myth.[9] But on the other hand, a whole research literature documents the decisive importance of local educators in implementing or, more likely, resisting innovations and reforms mandated from above.[10] The difficulty is that these two strands of literature are seldom integrated into one comprehensive view of the local policy context of public schools. Experts recognize that the contradiction between the two strands is more apparent than real, yet much of the literature fails to clarify this fact. Thus, on the first point, we are told that school boards and local educators and citizens have lost all but trivial influence over educational policy. And, indeed, abundant evidence exists that the scope of local decision-making power *at the school board level* has been vastly reduced since the 1960s, as federal and state constraints on policymaking have increased. Yet at the same time there is no doubt about the pivotal role of local educators in determining the extent to which new policies will be implemented *at the school and classroom level.*

In introductory courses in political science, we learn that the ability successfully to veto policies one opposes—at some point in the policy cycle, from policy formation to policy implementation—is a fundamental display of power, the obverse of the ability successfully to initiate a policy proposal. Clearly, this veto power is a resource that "powerless" educators seem to possess from coast to coast, regardless of variation in the degree of state-level initiative and power over educational policy. Of course, it usually is a "pocket veto," carried out quietly behind the classroom door. But, if anything, this approach makes it more effective than dramatic public confrontations that might arouse a lethargic citizenry.

Of the two competing bodies of research, that demonstrating the power of school-level educators over the fate of new programs and policies is far better documented and, consequently, more convincing. Moreover, while there can be no doubt that local control by school boards has been severely eroded, a significant residue remains in many states. Though further imperiled by rapidly increasing state centralization of power over school policy, in many places school districts still make some consequential choices about the character of the services they provide.[11] To see that this is true, one has only to compare American schools with those in most other countries, where highly centralized control of education is common. Of course, this is not to say that all is well with local control of schools. Indeed, it is the widely shared perception that local school authorities have failed to demand high standards that has promoted today's trend toward vastly increased state-level control of educational policy.[12] Consequently, both the concept and the reality of local control are very much in question and both certainly will remain issues in today's context of school reform.

When it comes to illuminating the context of reform, however, much of the literature on educational politics is not very helpful because of its schizophrenic tendency to point in incompatible directions. The literature emphasizing the weakness or even absence of local influences suggests that a top-down, "command and control" approach to educational policy and management is bound to succeed. What could impede it? But the implementation literature argues strongly that top-down approaches are misguided. What is needed instead, it counsels, is a bottom-up approach involving local adaptation of reform ideas.[13] Rather than "command and control," it says that a "beseech and facilitate" approach is far more likely to work.[14]

Amnesia and Ignorance in School Politics

Despite the extensive attention given to research findings about implementation problems for the past ten years, most of the education commission reports are written as though this vast body of knowledge never existed. Taking a top-down rather than bottom-up approach to the implementation of national and statewide educational reform, the commission reports— and most of the state plans resulting from them—blithely ignore the critical role played by local educators in accepting or rejecting innovations.

Some may feel the commissions really believed there were no local influences on schools or that they just "forgot" the implementation lessons of the 1970s. It seems far more likely, however, that many commissioners were unaware of the issues or evidence on the subject. Similarly, many reform-minded groups and state legislators have acted in ignorance of what we have learned about implementing change in schools. At the least, one might have expected some discussion of the competing research evidence and theories about changing schools before people pushed ahead to enact comprehensive statewide reform plans. This approach rarely has happened. Under the spell of folk heroes, such as H. Ross Perot in Texas, some states even have tended toward a sort of "Rambo" model of school reform.[15] Such heavy-handed attempts to ram reform down teachers' throats, and to test and closely monitor teacher performance, fly in the face of the findings of the implementation literature, not to mention research on teaching and modern theories of management.[16]

As James Guthrie has noted, "Fundamental components of the reform strategy seem to be painfully at odds with the dynamics of organizational revitalization."[17] The emphasis of the national commission reports, as Paula F. Silver observed, "is on changing the schools from *without* by mandating changes in the requirements, procedures, position titles, and/or accountability processes of schools."[18] But this approach generally neglects the *internal* workings of schools and what we've learned from the "effective schools" movement. Instead, "The new state 'initiatives' address such factors as length of school day, course title requirements, certification procedures . . . and the rituals of supervising instruction."[19] Thus, some reform policies are helpful and highly visible but leave untouched much of what goes on in schools. Other policies attempt to alter behavior in schools but without coming to grips with the essential underlying organizational dynamics. In this latter vein, the "excellence" reforms in some states represent an unprecedented attempt to reach into the classroom in a highly directive way to change the character of curriculum and instruction.[20] The weight of much research suggests such attempts at best will have mixed results.[21]

Of course, ignorance about school politics has become almost as American as apple pie. The apolitical legacy endowed upon public education by the nonpartisan reform movement seems to live on, rising like a phoenix from the flames of confrontations in the 1960s and 1970s that dramatically revealed the political issues at stake in schooling arrangements. All too often, leaders in education continue to manifest a technocratic attitude and are surprised and unprepared for the implications of demographic trends, the baby bust, the politics of retrenchment, and the like.

Obviously, the great danger of the current admixture of schizophrenia and ignorance in educational reform policy is that ballyhooed, but misguided, top-down reforms may backfire. If they do, the result will be further disillusionment with public education, increasing existing sentiment to abandon the public schools and support policies facilitating the privatization of education. Whether we can sustain the momentum of the current reform movement is the critical question confronting us.

It is hard to know just how widespread and intense teacher opposition to the various statewide reforms is, but it is clear that the major education professional groups have been against most of the reforms that have come in the wake of the *Nation at Risk* crisis. In a thoughtful review of recent case studies of seven of the leading "reform" states, Allan Odden concludes that "the lack of enthusiasm of the education community and outright opposition by elements within the community to nearly all of the proposed education reforms is a consistent theme."[22] This opposition by the key institutional interest groups makes the progress to date of the current reform movement all the more remarkable. A key element in this debate at the state level, Odden notes, has been the insistence by state politicians that more dollars for education would be forthcoming only in exchange for acceptance of reforms. Indeed, in Texas, H. Ross Perot used as his slogan, "Millions for reform, but not one dime for the status quo."[23]

But acceptance of reforms at the legislative level scarcely assures faithful implementation at the school and classroom level. If effective implementation depends to some degree on positive attitudes on the part of implementors—and it certainly must—then the evidence so far is disconcerting. Consider, first, that a national poll in 1986 showed that teachers have far less positive attitudes about current reforms than do leaders in the reform movement, that is, governors, education school deans, and union leaders.[24] Second, this aggregate finding is strongly supported by reports coming out of states like Texas and Tennessee. For example, a survey of Knox County, Tennessee, teachers, conducted by proponents of the state's Better Schools Program, found overwhelming disapproval of the program. More than 90 percent of the 900 teachers surveyed indicated either that they "strongly disagreed" or "disagreed" with statements that "The Better Schools Program has boosted teacher morale to a professional level"; that "The Better Schools Program has been viewed by teachers as successful across the state"; and that "The major emphasis of the Better Schools Program is on the quality of instruction rather than recordkeeping, evaluation, and recording portfolios by the teachers."[25]

Next consider the case of Utah. In carefully researched studies of decision making on career-ladder plans in the legislature and in school districts, B. Malen and A. W. Hart document how "the distinctive features of a career ladder (promotional positions and differentiated salaries) are being compromised *at all levels* of the system. With few exceptions, the reform is being converted into familiar practice."[26] They show that a great deal of ingenuity is being used to defeat the intent of career ladders, through such techniques as secrecy about who gets the promotions and "rotating promotions" or "step ladders," that is, "you step up and you step down."[27]

Apart from the reaction of teachers, policies being pursued in the name of excellence often reflect a further ironic dimension of ignorance about school policy and politics: they frequently are at odds with both the contemporary implications of educational excellence and the conditions necessary for it. In an attempt to "mandate excellence" and "legislate learning," most states have enacted statewide policies that centralize control and standardize the character of public schooling.[28] Yet for many people excellence in education requires diversity and choice in schooling arrangements.

In general, there has been widespread failure in the educational establishment to appreciate how the politics of excellence tend to promote demands for choice that will reconfigure educational politics and management. Terrel Bell has warned that parental demands for choice among schools and teachers will grow. He notes that schools "are the last bastion of regulated and controlled services" and predicts that the trend toward deregulation in many industries will reach education in the next three to five years.[29] Although the National Governors Association report, *Time for Results,* also endorses greater choice in schooling, most school administrators appear insensitive to this trend or reluctant to acknowledge it. Instead, they cling to the administrative tradition and convenience of the norm of "universalism" and the "one best system" approach to the provision of schooling.[30]

If most of the reformers guiding the excellence movement have been afflicted by amnesia and ignorance about school politics, it also is true that scholars in the field have not escaped a share of these maladies. Few scholars were prepared for the Reagan administration's far-reaching success in exhortation or "sermonizing from the 'bully pulpit'" to reshape educational policy priorities.[31] It seems we had nearly forgotten about the importance of leadership and symbolic politics. Further, scholars tolerated and abetted ignorance in the field by failing to resolve the tension between the competing schools of thought about managing change, that is, between the extremes of the "command and control" and "beseech and facilitate" approaches. We might have been able to head off some of our problems with extremes of "top-downism" if we had achieved a persuasive synthesis to guide policymakers. Even at this late date it seems worthwhile to pursue this goal.

Command versus Beseech: Toward a Synthesis

The great difficulty with much of the literature emphasizing barriers to implementation and local adaptation of innovations is that it implies that one can only get educators to do what they already want to do. Such an approach seems to preclude significant reform. However, recent research on the cumulative or longitudinal effects of federal reform efforts and on the "bully pulpit" strategy shows that more than a fragile bottom-up, "mutual adaptation" approach to educational reform can work. This new body of research underscores the importance of leadership, of new and persuasive symbols, and of reform and change as forms of organizational learning or resocialization. It shows how, when, and what kind of top-down strategies can be effective.

Obviously, the effective use of top-down strategies requires care and sophistication. As beleaguered "street-level bureaucrats," educators need much more than just exhortation and prodding; they also need positive incentives, support, resources, and self-respect.[32] Heavy-handed attempts to ensure excellence by pressuring pedagogues most likely will misfire. For example, L. M. McNeil describes how new requirements in Texas are "deskilling" teachers and driving out exactly the kind of persons we need to attract and retain to upgrade the profession.[33]

By briefly reviewing the literature on the competing management approaches, we can see the strengths and weaknesses of each and gain insights about how top-down and bottom-up strategies may balance and complement one another. In this way, we can begin to delineate a balanced approach to educational improvement, using elements of each strategy judiciously according to the characteristics and needs of the given policy problem. Rather than succumbing to the temptations of either-or thinking, we need to recognize the parallel with the claim of T. J. Peters and R. H. Waterman, Jr., that excellent companies were characterized by "simultaneous loose-tight properties." That is, they were "both centralized and decentralized" and distinguished by "the coexistence of firm central direction and maximum individual autonomy."[34] The firm central direction sets the key values and parameters that guide activity, but the sphere of activity has an openness that encourages individual initiative and creativity. Analysis of the recent literature on educational policy and on management suggests that the optimum approach in school reform also would be characterized by "simultaneous loose-tight properties."

In pursuit of a synthesis of competing approaches, we could

start by viewing social and educational reform as problems of redistribution. Difficulties in reform seem to revolve around two kinds of redistribution: substantive and psychic. Social policies aimed at remedying inequities, at aiding the disadvantaged, are obviously and substantively redistributive. Such policies clearly lead a constrained and precarious existence in market-oriented societies concerned with efficiency and productivity. But new policies and programs that require service delivery personnel to abandon familiar and comfortable routines to benefit someone else also are redistributive, even if only psychic costs are involved. When a unilateral imposition of costs on semiprofessionals occurs, they also experience a loss in autonomy and self-respect on top of other costs. Moreover, much more may be at stake than just psychic costs and the violation of the "psychological contract" with the employer.[35] Employees may well feel they are being deprived of a real "property right" they have in their job. For example, this deprivation seems clearly the case when the seniority-based compensation system of teachers is jeopardized by merit-pay and career-ladder plans. Finally, it is important to note that reforms often alter power relationships within and between organizations. Thus, one of the significant effects of reforms may be to redistribute influence.

The importance for successful innovation of adaptation and of a bottom-up management approach was driven home by the influential Rand Change Agent study, published in an eight-volume report series called *Federal Programs Supporting Educational Change*. This large-scale study of federally funded innovative projects drew data primarily from a survey of 293 projects and follow-up case studies of 29 of the programs. The findings emphasized the importance of local problem-solving capacity and local adaptation in the implementation of innovations. The study's main themes—that nonimplementation is common and that successful implementation depends upon a bottom-up process of "mutual adaptation" at the school site level, in which case both the innovation and the school site practices are modified—substantially influenced the thinking of analysts and, to some degree, policymakers also.

What is required is a policy and management approach that

focuses on building adaptive schools and social service organizations by fostering professional problem-solving capacity within them. R. F. Elmore argues that, rather than attempts to maximize hierarchical control and compliance, the inescapable complexity and concomitant professional discretion involved in social services require an approach that fosters the capacity to deliver the service.[36] Consequently, instead of hierarchical control,

> The skillful use of delegated control is central to making implementation work in bottom-heavy, loosely coupled systems. *When it becomes necessary to rely mainly on hierarchical control, regulation, and compliance to achieve results, the game is essentially lost.* Moving from delegated control to hierarchical control means moving from reliance on existing capacity, ingenuity, and judgment [on the part of service delivery personnel] to reliance on rules, surveillance, and enforcement procedures. Regulation increases complexity and invites subversion; it diverts attention from accomplishing the task to understanding and manipulating the rules.[37]

Consistent with Elmore's assessment, other analysts have concluded that "to manage is not to control" but rather to get results, performance, desired outcomes. The idea that the focus in "bottom-heavy, loosely coupled" organizations should be on getting results—via extensive use of delegated rather than hierarchical control to build performance capacity—clearly has far-reaching implications for educational policy and management. A delegated-control approach reduces the "psychic costs" problem of implementation and reform for professionals by generating incentives of professional collaboration, pride, and ownership over policies and programs that professionals have adapted to meet their circumstances and needs. The trick, of course, is to provide leadership that respects educators as professionals but nevertheless motivates substantial change and improvement. Frequently, more than fragile, bottom-up mutual adaptation is needed. And, indeed, recent research and policy developments show that more is possible.

What seems to work is a strategy similar to that which appears fruitful in dealing with the more politically difficult side of the redistribution problem: the enactment and implementation of substantively redistributive policies. Peterson argues persuasively that, rather than employing highly specific and prescriptive directives that conflict with local needs for flexibility and adaptation, effective leadership can be proffered through actions that set, propagate, maintain, and legitimate goals and minimum standards for the organization and, more broadly, for the just society. Such an approach encourages organizational learning over time through an evolutionary process, one in which local and state authorities and constituency groups begin to internalize and identify with the goals that are set and monitored.

In the final analysis, it is clear that neither bottom-up mutual adaptation nor top-down bully pulpitism will suffice by itself. Rather, we need a balanced approach using elements of each strategy sensitively, according to the characteristics and needs of the given policy problem. As Peterson demonstrates, substantively redistributive policies usually will require top-down mandates and monitoring whereas policies enhancing broadly shared local interests ("developmental" policies in his terms) will be less likely to require top-down enforcement (and more likely to thrive under mutual adaptation).[38]

If we hope to translate vision into reality, we have to have a sophisticated plan for *systemic* organizational change that takes full account of implementation problems. This is where crude, top-down approaches get into trouble. By themselves, mandates and exhortations from the bully pulpit are scarcely enough to produce fundamental and lasting change.

Happily, there now are signs that simplistic, top-down approaches are beginning to be replaced with more substantive efforts aimed at restructuring and transforming fundamental characteristics of public schools and the teaching profession. At the forefront of the "second wave" of reform are the efforts of the Carnegie Forum, the Holmes Group, and the National Governors Association. The influential reports of these three groups—*A Nation Prepared: Teachers for the 21st Century; Tomorrow's Teachers;* and *Time for Results: The Governors' 1991 Report on Education,* respectively—represent a comprehensive and far-reaching agenda for reform and revitalization of the nation's public schools. Significantly, substantial areas of agreement occur among the three reports. Moreover, the three groups recognize that they need to collaborate as a coalition for effective reform, and the national teachers' unions, the NEA and the AFT, have endorsed the Carnegie report. What remains to be seen is just how much the site-level implementors—teachers and school administrators—will buy into this second wave of reform and see it as a desirable development for their professions.

Clearly, some tricky issues must be negotiated here. One of the stickiest involves the new relationships necessary between teachers and administrators if teachers are to play a larger role in professional decision making. Another challenging issue is associated with the increasing recognition of the need for measures to enhance parental choice among public schools. Closely related, as part of the second wave effort to revitalize the performance and career and incentive structures for teachers and school administrators, is the need to break up the complacent, consumer-insensitive, monopoly relationship that public schools enjoy in relation to most of their clients. As B. R. Clark and others argue, the latter two goals can be advanced by fostering curriculum variety and differentiation among public schools and then competition among them for clients.[39] Indeed, former governor of Minnesota Albert H. Quie contends: "If teachers are to be allowed more discretion, then parents should be permitted to select from among the different programs developed by professionals. The moves for expanded educator professionalism and increased parental choice among schools are inextricably bound together."[40]

In the final analysis, successful school reform will require the kind of balanced approach outlined above—one characterized by "simultaneous loose-tight properties"—and persistence. Without leadership at the state and federal levels in setting key values and parameters, local schools are inclined to drift and respond mainly to localized values. Although instructionally effective schools and school districts appear to have schemes of controls that are tighter than usual, even these high performers are not characterized by extremes of top-down prescription and dictation.[41] The reality of professional work in publicly controlled and funded schools requires a compromise between professional and bureaucratic models of control. Neither the entirely professionalized nor the entirely bureaucratized model is workable or desirable. Moreover, because parents and the public at large can be frozen out, even from a compromise of these two models, there is concern for maintaining and enhancing hybrid models that combine politics and markets along with elements of professionalism and bureaucracy. The most immediate problem for the current reform movement, however, is to resolve the mounting tension between calls for increased professionalization of teaching and the reality of rapidly growing state-level dictation of the specifics of curriculum and instruction.

Whatever the resolution of these issues, reform requires persistence because time is necessary for attitude change and organizational learning. Indeed, J. G. March and J. P. Olsen argue that reorganization and reform often succeed in the long run, despite short-run failures, precisely because of the poser of their rhetoric and symbols to change the climate of opinion over time. Thus, they observe that "reorganization can be viewed as a form of civic education."[42] Fortunately, the "window of opportunity" for American educational reform has remained open longer than originally expected. The challenge before us is to make the most of it.

Conclusion

The turbulent, demanding environment facing public schools today clearly requires responsive, skilled, and informed leadership by policymakers and public educators. A continuation of the kind of schizophrenia, amnesia, and ignorance we have seen in school politics could contribute to the downfall of public schools as broadly supported, democratic institutions. The present adverse combination of demographic, sociopolitical, and economic trends will require more of the public schools than just business as usual, muddling through, and massive inertia. To avoid decline, public educators will have to adapt and cope creatively with their challenging environment. And policymakers will need to avoid the extremes of top-down and bottom-up policy approaches. With the proper approach, a truly collaborative and effective process for school improvement can emerge. In this endeavor, dissemination of better knowledge about the realities of school reform and school politics can play an important part in producing the leadership and policies required for this "first real crisis" in public education.

Bill Clinton and Arkansas: Can Political Leaders Reform the Schools?

ROBERT W. JOHNS

On July 14, 1987, Bill Clinton, Arkansas's youthful Rhodes Scholar governor, surprised even some of his closest friends and aides by announcing that he would not seek the office of president of the United States. Two days later in what the *Arkansas Gazette* called "an emotionally charged press conference" at the splendid new Excelsior Hotel in Little Rock, the governor spoke of his obligation to his family, especially his seven-year-old daughter. Still, he suggested that his time might yet come, saying, "For whatever it's worth, I'd still like to be President." Clinton's trips around the country to "test the waters," he reported, had led him to conclude that the time was ripe, but his heart, he said, was somehow not in it.

Bill Clinton's national political aspirations and the public perception of the success of public school reforms in Arkansas have been directly linked. During the mid-1980s his political star rose and shone brightly as he rode a national wave of so-called educational reform. His star appeared to dim considerably in 1989, especially when he failed to get the legislature—in both regular and special sessions—to appropriate sufficient funds to continue paying for the "reforms." Until then, however, his success was heady stuff for a bright, ambitious young governor. He initiated a variety of education mandates and achieved national attention through his proposal, later approved by the General Assembly, that current teachers pass a state test on communication and mathematical skills and knowledge of subject or lose their jobs. Under attack by the Arkansas Education Association on his teacher-testing proposal, he often protested that he had proposed a comprehensive program and that he knew that real reform would require more than testing. In November 1986, during the time he was chairman of the National Governors Association Task Force on Leadership and Management, he wrote in the *Phi Delta Kappan* that a second "wave of reform" would be required to sustain the reform mandates: "Strong leaders create strong schools. Both research and common sense suggest that administrators can do a great deal to advance school reform. They will lead the next wave of reform, and states and governors must act now to help them lead."[1]

Clinton's talk of a second "wave of reform" and of "strong leaders" who could, he supposed, "create strong schools" turned out to be neither political overstatement nor idle chatter. During his successful reelection campaign in 1986, he was impressed by teachers' complaints about being deluged with bureaucratic paperwork designed to demonstrate compliance with the new standards that he had pushed through the legislature in 1983. In 1987, the governor began to refer in public to such things as a "second wave" of reform, "bureaucratic" paperwork that reduced time for teaching, "higher order learning," and "restructuring schools." In December 1987, he and the state superintendent of education, Dr. Ruth Steele, convened a two-day conference in Little Rock, "Schools for Arkansas's Future: Restructuring for Higher Order Learning," to which they invited representatives of fifteen public school districts that had "fully met" the standards by the fall 1987 deadline.

On the eve of the conference, as a guest writer in a column in the Sunday *Arkansas Gazette* on December 13, the governor pointed with pride to the "impressive and commendable" school reforms he claimed had been implemented since *Nation at Risk* and state mandates of 1983, but he said, "Clearly, a second wave of reform" was necessary.[2] He said that the "second wave" must include "restructuring" relationships between the state and schools, principals, and teachers to promote the development of information-processing skills demanded in a high-tech world. He noted the lack of agreement about what "restructuring" means, but he proceeded to identify everything from decentralizing state and school decision making to collaboration with social agencies to reduce dropouts and from early childhood programs for the disadvantaged to rejection of "the teacher as repository-of-facts." He said that the fifteen districts invited to the conference would have the opportunity to hear national leaders and devise their own experiments with restructuring.

Clinton opened the conference by repeating what he had said in the column. He was not content merely to serve in his official role as conference chairperson but from the outset participated as if he knew as much about education as his nationally known panel, which included Theodore Sizer, Michael Cohen, and Marc Tucker. He was scheduled to continue as chairperson on the second day of the conference, but a tornado struck West Memphis, and he left the meeting to assess the damage. In order to open the meeting in the first place, Clinton had had to hurry back from Washington, D.C., where, as president of the National Forum for Youth at Risk and immediate past chairman of the Education Commission of the States (ECS), he had released the results of an ECS survey on dropouts among the disadvantaged. Only a natural disaster, it seems, could keep him from education's center stage.

Purpose

My purpose in this chapter is to describe and evaluate school reform in Arkansas during the 1980s, including Governor Clinton's key role. Because by 1990 the so-called second wave and restructuring were still in embryonic form (and being pursued in only 29 of the state's 329 school districts), I will include here only a brief assessment of that type of initiative's potential. My thesis is that the essentially top-down, regulatory, and punitive pattern of reform in Arkansas, which has not been successful elsewhere, was largely unsuccessful in Arkansas in the 1980s and cannot be expected to succeed in Arkansas in the long term—indeed, may even result in a net loss. Research on federal and state initiatives, including the early returns on Arkansas, clearly indicates that success in such top-down "reform" is unlikely because it distorts the curriculum, obscures the real staff development needs, and does not take into account crucial characteristics of the culture of effective schools (especially teacher efficacy, the unique aspects of each school, and the long-enculturated pattern of schooling).

To develop my thesis, I describe the course and fate of the efforts to implement Arkansas's major reform mandates during the 1980s and weigh their chances of long-term success, primarily in the light of research on the following: (1) the deep structure of schooling nationwide and the unique personality of each school; (2) effective schools; (3) centrally mandated reforms; and (4) past reform movements, including those in other states. I briefly evaluate the restructuring proposal and point to an exceptional opportunity for success, the small school— the dominant type in Arkansas. Although some instances of success did run counter to the predominant mandate pattern, I refer to them largely to illustrate, or to suggest ways to remedy, deficiencies in the Arkansas reform efforts of the 1980s.

Description

Two state-level initiatives set the tone, direction, and boundaries for school reform in Arkansas during the 1980s: (1) the General Assembly's 1983 bill, signed into law by Clinton, that required teachers to pass a test on "functional academic skills and knowledge of subject area" by June 1987 or lose their certification; and (2) *Standards for Accreditation of Arkansas Public Schools,* proposed by a committee chaired by Hillary Clinton, the governor's wife, under the General Assembly's "Quality Education Act" (1983) and adopted by the State Board of Education in February 1984. Schools had to meet these standards by the 1987–88 school year or expect to be consolidated with schools that had met the standards.

Advocates of these initiatives appear to have presupposed that *more is better,* including more requirements, more standardized testing, and more courses in academic subject fields.

All teachers, students, and schools were directly affected. Certified teachers had to pass basic English, mathematics, and teaching specialty tests or expect to lose their jobs. Students had to pass eighth-grade tests in English, mathematics, science, and social studies or expect not to be promoted to high school. Schools had to offer a minimum of thirty-eight units (up from twenty-four), hire more counselors, add more school days and hours in the school day, hire more teachers to reduce the teacher-student ratio in classes at all levels, and meet many other essentially quantitative changes or expect consolidation with other schools. Beyond that, any school or school district in which at least 85 percent of its students in the third, sixth, and eighth grades did not meet minimum performance levels specified by the state were to be consolidated with another school or school district—unless "reasonable progress" was achieved in a two-year improvement program.

In the period between the 1983 enactment and the 1987 deadline for implementation, the new standards were greeted with a mixture of praise and criticism, resistance and support. Most teachers across the state felt demoralized—professionally demeaned—because they felt left out of the process of deciding upon the new standards and, as professional educators, insulted by having to pass tests on "basics" to retain their certification.[3] Despite the fact that not only teachers but most students and administrators reported a substantial increase in stress and anxiety, school districts generally supported the changes.[4] Through it all, the state board, supported by the governor and the state education department, held the line and persevered. The board held hearings at several points with administrators from each district to indicate the status of their compliance and to explain what steps, if any, would be necessary to meet the standards fully.

Most districts mobilized themselves to do many things that previously they could not—or would not—do for themselves, such as find new monies, offer a comprehensive curriculum, hire new teachers to staff it and to reduce teacher-student ratios, arrange to share specialists and resources with neighboring districts, and voluntarily consolidate with other districts. Between 1983 and 1990, thirty-two districts voluntarily consolidated. Not a single district was forcibly consolidated by the state board, though four were put on probation at one point.

Support for implementing the new (1983) standards came from many directions. The state education department organized many supporting conferences, notably meetings of selected classroom teachers to develop course content guides that identified minimal and enrichment "skills" targeted for each course. In many districts, superintendents, sometimes acting at the prompting of classroom teachers, took advantage of the in-service support of one of the state's sixteen regional educational cooperatives (e.g., to help elementary teachers deal with additional science or art requirements). Similarly, a small number of initiatives came from universities to help teachers develop sound curriculum plans (e.g., for a new course, "Survey of the Fine Arts," which requires knowledge and perspectives from several disciplines).

Beginning in 1984, a particularly exemplary initiative was organized that joined university and state education department personnel with teachers, representatives of some of the educational cooperatives, and interested lay citizens. The effort was mounted by the Arkansas International Center (AIC) at the University of Arkansas at Little Rock in cooperation with the state social studies specialist, Cheryl Pagan. Pagan, together with Susan Wilkes and Walter Nunn of the AIC, organized a consortium of teachers, teacher educators, subject field specialists, and community representatives that developed a long-term plan and obtained Danforth Foundation support to prepare teachers for the mandated course offering, "Global Studies." By 1990, this collaborative effort, under the continuing leadership of the AIC, was still growing, with the consortium having become the Arkansas Council on Global Education (ACOGE). The AIC and the ACOGE network supports local team efforts to infuse global perspectives into schools and communities, particularly collaborations between the school, university, and private sectors. Unfortunately, nonhierarchical collaboration, like that launched through the global education consortium, was the exception rather than the rule during the

1980s. By 1990, similar and potentially long-term university support for teachers in meeting the state standards was developing around the state, partly in response to new standards from the National Council for the Accreditation of Teacher Education (which called for closer university-school relationships).

Although the typical reaction by most educators to the new standards was to attempt to comply and to seek the necessary financial and staff development support, there were, at the outset, notable exceptions. Perhaps the most explosive response, certainly the biggest media event, was the reaction by certified teachers to teacher testing. Governor Clinton was determined not to roll back the requirement despite pressures from the community and from state legislators and despite legal threats and actions by the Arkansas Education Association (AEA). The AEA came forth with an evaluation plan that included systematic observation of instruction, but it was apparently too late in the public debate for the governor to retreat. Early administrations of the test included a number of bizarre and embarrassing developments (e.g., a test was stolen on one occasion prior to the testing hour, and on another occasion the governor had a private meeting with then–State Superintendent of Education Tommy R. Venters regarding his permitting the test to be given in his office to avoid embarrassing a local superintendent). Subsequent test administrations, however, were generally proper and orderly affairs. State education offices released figures on several occasions that indicated that about 90 percent of the teachers passed the test and that black teachers were disproportionately represented among those who failed it. Teachers who failed the test—or did not take it—had to achieve acceptable scores on six hours of the National Teacher Examination and six semester credit hours of advanced work in their teaching field in order to retain certification.

A potentially even more explosive development than teacher testing that looms on the horizon is student testing—for third, sixth, and eighth graders. Although the "minimum performance tests" (MPT) on "basic" subjects had been administered by the state education department since 1985, in the spring of

1988 eighth graders were required, for the first time, to pass the tests in order to enter high school. The anxiety levels of eighth-grade teachers and students were exceptionally high despite the fact that students could receive remedial help during the summer and might take the test up to two more times. Given the governor's commitment to both higher standards and higher office, dealing with the eighth-grade test results appeared, in 1988, to be one of the toughest challenges he had faced. Within a year, however, Winthrop Rockefeller Foundation researchers found a 90 + percent pass-rate in almost every school district in Arkansas. In fact, in most districts only a handful of students failed even the first administration of the MPT; the state had set up a test that was, as one superintendent said, "very, very minimum."[5]

Clinton had escaped a potential political crisis, but the multiple side effects brought by the MPT threatened to reduce to zero—or less—the gains of the "first wave" of reform that he had so strongly espoused. A massive, three-year study by the Rockefeller Foundation (1985–88), which included in-depth case studies of fifteen districts representative of state public schools as a whole, clearly indicated that the MPT had been the key cause or catalyst for the following developments: (1) unwarranted reclassification of many junior high students into special education; (2) distortion of the curriculum so that the minimum tended to become the maximum (i.e., instruction tended to focus almost entirely on the minimum competencies identified in mandated course content guides); (3) substantial reduction in instruction for higher-level understanding and thinking abilities; (4) increased neglect of the academic needs of the largest group, the so-called average students; and (5) a substantial decrease in time spent on stimulating interest, enjoyment of the learning process, and creative activities.[6] Of course, all of these responses to implementation of the MPT tended to be exaggerated at the mandatory testing levels— grades three, six, and eight.

Among most teachers, negative responses to teacher and student testing extended to the reform movement in general. Governor Clinton's failure to obtain funds from the General

Assembly in its 1989 sessions was seen by most teachers as just another demoralizing and frustrating event in a long line that began with teacher testing and extended to broken promises regarding salary and other funding increases and to the extraordinary amount of paperwork required to demonstrate compliance with standards. Although bureaucratic paperwork varied across school systems, in one district near Little Rock, selected to participate in the state-initiated "restructuring for higher order learning", experiment, elementary teachers were required to write into every lesson plan they taught—presumably several each day—how the lessen plan contributed to achieving one or more of the mandated "basic skills." In another district, a sixth-grade teacher's comment epitomized the frustration felt by teachers: "I have 191 skills to teach to my sixth graders. I know there's no way we will get through it all."[7]

By the third year of the Rockefeller Foundation's case study interviews (fall 1988), all groups—teachers, administrators, community members, members of the board, even students— acknowledged the presence and key role of low teacher morale and lack of participation in decision making: "The case study respondents universally agreed that the lack of widespread teacher involvement in planning, writing and implementing the standards has led to diminished self-respect and a weaker commitment to the reforms among teachers."[8]

Dr. Sara Murphy, principal investigator for the Rockefeller study, noted that by the late 1980s teachers had generally come not even to trust state-level initiatives at all.[9] She said that this mistrust resulted when low morale due to lack of involvement in deciding reforms was compounded by (a) the state's failure to deliver promised salary increases and (b) the widespread teacher perception that the standards were funded from teacher salaries, the largest item in the state budget.

Yet, despite the negative responses of many teachers across the state, positive reactions to the standards and signs of hope for real reform did occur. Besides the almost universally welcomed reduction in teacher-student ratios at all levels, substantial support existed for the mandate for more courses. The more progressive superintendents in small districts, while over-worked and financially overburdened (due to a shortfall in state revenue), found that the new standards had given them the leverage they needed with the community to bring in new ideas and a more comprehensive program. Further, meeting the new standards often made small district staffs feel a part of a sound and special movement, and the threat of consolidation provided a unifying effect in the community. As one principal noted: "It's affected the community because they think if we lose our school, we'll lose our community. They will get in-volved if threatened with the loss of the school. If everything else goes fine then they do not get involved much." Unfortu-nately, the needed increase in community and parental support for school reforms, experienced by many small districts threat-ened by consolidation, was not generally to be found across the state during the 1980s.[10]

Administrators in small, rural districts also experienced various frustrations with the "first wave of reform." Because many such districts rely too heavily on a small- or medium-sized farm economy that lacks capital and has suffered severe losses in the past decade, they were unable to carry out reforms as fully as they had hoped—or were expected—to do. Ener-getic, progressive administrators were doubly frustrated when promised state revenue was not delivered after their commu-nities had taxed themselves to the maximum. They were also often discouraged when they, like their urban counterparts, saw their best and most creative teachers being harnessed to textbooks and required basic skills.[11] By the end of the 1980s, in small schools as well as large, most educators across Arkan-sas felt frustrated and discouraged (although they found reason to believe that, somehow, constructive change was still possi-ble).

Analysis of the "First Wave"

So, can the state standards that became law in 1983 be suc-cessful? And, can political leaders make them work? Because 1987–88 was the first full year in which the new standards had to be in place, it may take five or six years before we can be sure. Nevertheless, evidence from other times and places, as well as the returns on development in Arkansas described previously, provide substantial reasons to believe that the answer to both questions is a flat, "no" (although there are areas where hope is still justifiable, particularly for small schools and the small-school concept). First let us look at the negative indicators. Generally speaking, the first wave of reforms is not likely to succeed or last because *it does not reflect sufficient consideration of* (1) the deep structure of schools and the unique personality of each school;[12] (2) the relationship between learning facts and learning to use them;[13] (3) characteristics of "good" or "effective" schools;[14] and (4) lessons from the nation's past reform movements, national and state.[15] I discuss each of these points in turn, followed by a consideration of the future of education reform in Arkansas, including a brief discussion of "restructuring" and the potential of supporting, rather than consolidating, the small school.

(1) *Deep Structure/Unique Personality:* Barbara Tye, in a representative sample of high schools for the Study of Schooling series, found a "deep structure of schooling" in every case that included the following elements: physical uniformity of classroom arrangement (desks in rows facing front toward the teacher); an overall emphasis upon control in curriculum, methods, and policies; tracking of students; very similar program and teaching practices; and a dependency upon tests for measuring success.[16] She points out that this deep structure rests upon deeply held values that have been internalized since colonial times, so that any change in it is likely to be met with strong resistance from all constituents—students as well as staff and community. For example, the student agitations for more freedom and participation in decision making in schools and colleges in the late 1960s promised a change, but Tye found in the late 1970s that the deep structure was still in place.

(2) *Learning Basic Facts and Using Them:* The focus of the "first wave of reform" in Arkansas upon teaching basic skills and information fits the long-term pattern Tye found nationwide. In Arkansas, as elsewhere, then, one does not need to go

"back to basics"; schools have never left them. This emphasis on so-called basics is a problem not only because it has such a long history that it is now encrusted in the curriculum and resistant to change but also because, according to long-established research, even basic facts cannot be remembered—much less used effectively in the information processing required in our times—unless they are combined in images and ideas that are meaningful or useful to students.[17] For these reasons it will take a great deal of effort from political leaders, as well as practitioners, at local, state, and perhaps even national levels to break through the deep structure's resistance to more than basic facts and skills.

(3) *Characteristics of Effective Schools:* The "first wave" of reform in Arkansas, implementation of the 1983 standards, has been top-down, regulatory, and punitive—the same for all schools with no deviations allowed except for temporary, probationary ones. But as Tye has pointed out, lasting reform tends to take place school by school because each school has, besides the common deep structure, a unique configuration of personalities, values, relationships, and resources—what she calls its "unique personality." Only through this unique personality can change be achieved. Tye's construct is confirmed by other research that shows that effective schools depend upon a strong sense of teacher ownership, or efficacy.[18] As previously indicated, most Arkansas teachers feel imposed upon, harnessed to textbooks and paperwork that they must do in order to demonstrate that the standards are being met. This procedure hardly respects teacher efficacy, does not allow unique aspects of each school's personality to be taken into account, and certainly does not take advantage of the sense of community found in so many small schools in Arkansas, a factor highly correlated with high achievement in the United States and abroad.[19]

The research conclusion that teacher efficacy and respect for the unique personality of each school are crucial to the success of schools and school improvement found clear support in the Arkansas experience of the 1980s. This fact is evident in the Rockefeller study's final conclusion that two central obstacles to success have been (a) the lack of involvement of teachers in decision making at every stage and (b) the lack of flexibility in implementing changes.[20]

(4) *Lessons From the Past—National and State:* The last academic reform movement, the one in response to Sputnik, was a failure except for a limited lasting influence on instruction in science. Like the first wave in Arkansas, the process of deciding upon and implementing curriculum changes following Sputnik had no place for input from the actual classroom teachers in each school or school district, that is, from those who must implement the reforms.[21]

Arkansas's political leaders also did not learn from the results of state-level reform efforts in other states during the late 1970s and early 1980s. In a summary of factors that have accompanied successful state reforms, Allan Odden and B. Anderson include the following: a district advocate who is not officially in a position of authority; external pressure for accountability; a fit between state plans and a local need *as it is perceived by the local district;* local cross-roll teams with discretionary authority and funds; state resources, technical and financial; and an overall conception of the changes being undertaken, as opposed to lists of skills, competencies, and objectives.[22] Except for state-level accountability pressure and a very limited amount of technical resources from one of the state's sixteen regional education cooperatives—which receive only $200,000 each annually—state leaders did not provide for these essentials of success. These six factors were not derived directly from Arkansas's experience. Nevertheless, they point to a failure.

There is, in fact, good reason to expect that the outcome of the first wave of reform in Arkansas will even be a net loss. This may be the case because tests are being used for student and teacher accountability. The kinds of distortions of curriculum resulting from using the minimum performance tests for accountability (described previously) are well known to education researchers. For example, Arthur E. Wise, director of the RAND Corporation's Center for the Study of the Teaching Profession, says that mandates from the government, like the new Arkansas standards, can solve problems of equity but not problems of quality. "Paradoxically," he says, "central mandates to improve the quality of education often reduce it."[23] This is the case, he contends, because teachers—often against their better judgment about what their students need—begin to distort and reduce the curriculum in order to emphasize what will be on the test. Arkansas's top-down, regulatory, and punitive approach to reform in the 1980s documents, once again, well-established research on school reform.

The reform mandates in Arkansas confronted both students and teachers with double messages, dilemmas they frequently could not resolve. For example, eighth-grade students were showered with messages not to be dropouts but were simultaneously faced with tests that both teachers and administrators knew many poor, minority students could not pass, increasing the likelihood of their dropping out. Likewise, teachers who knew that "higher order learning" is integral to "lower order learning" (and vice versa) were faced with lists of competencies that they did not devise and had no time—in some cases no expertise—to integrate into a conceptually meaningful whole that would enable them to do much more than teach to the low-level, minimum-competency test. The result was that neither level of cognitive objectives was likely to get accomplished very well, lower or higher. Beyond these dilemmas for both student and teacher was the increasing potential for them to develop the sense of powerlessness, loss of community, and alienation that lies beneath so many problems in the education system and the society at large. One wonders if the Deep Southern, and Arkansan, sense of community can find the cultural and financial resources necessary to meet this challenge.

Conclusion:
Where Should Arkansas Go from Here?

Even if I did not believe that there is truth in the ideas of determinism, destiny, and deity, I would still have to wonder if the forces of fate are not directing the education reform efforts in Arkansas. The December 12 issue of the *Arkansas Gazette* reported that the State Department of Education had proposed "a sweeping reorganization of the state's school system to provide for extensive consolidation of school districts and units, reduction of administrative units and raising of teachers' salaries." That was December 12, *1937!* Fifty years later to the week, the *Gazette* carried an article reporting the governor's solemn pledge to obtain higher salaries for the state's teachers who are working to ward off the threat of consolidation.[24] Even educators who are the proud descendants of those who mastered the Arkansas wilderness, but who have experienced firsthand the pendular swings of so-called reform, may be tempted to agree with the conclusion of the Stoic philosopher-king, Marcus Aurelius, in the sunset years of the Greco-Roman civilization: "Everywhere up and down thou wilt find the same things, with which the old histories are filled. . . . There is nothing new; all things are both familiar and short-lived. . . . To have contemplated human life for forty years is the same as to have contemplated it for ten thousand years."[25]

To apply Marcus Aurelius's judgment to educational reform in Arkansas in the 1980s would perhaps be too severe and pessimistic. After all, his world preceded the so-called rise of the West—the scientific, technological, economic, and democratic revolutions that made Western culture dominant and is still changing the face and culture of Arkansas and the rest of the world. Nevertheless, one must hope that the long view—and the realization that proposals for restructuring were put forth by Arkansas political and education officials fifty years ago without much success—will give perspective and perhaps pause to current would-be reformers and their potential disciples. One who sees the need for significant school reform in Arkansas—as I do—must hope that reformers will notice in United States history the cyclical or pendular nature of proposed school overhauls and take seriously the mounting evidence supporting Barbara Tye's research and her identification of the unique personality of each school and the deep structure of schooling that is nationwide and has its origins in Puritan times.[26] Only then can reforms be more than marginally successful. Only then can political and education officials—as well as principals, students, teachers, and teacher educators—take their proper and special roles.

If political leaders are genuinely committed to lasting reform in Arkansas, then they will realize that making pronouncements and calling conferences in Little Rock *about* "restructuring for higher order learning" is not their most useful role. If the deep structural, nationwide pattern of control-oriented and teacher-centered classes that has tended to keep instruction on lower cognitive levels is to change, then they must take to the stump throughout the state. They must obtain in each community the essential private sector, higher education, and community fiscal and political support for team efforts in each school in order to develop and sustain new ways to engage all students in acquiring *and* using knowledge. But even more is needed. For the restructuring effort to achieve more than minimal success, the governor and the state education department will need a real dialogue, including participation in decision making, among all those who influence or are influenced by teacher decisions—in each school and at every stage of program development and implementation. To date such a participatory effort has not been mounted. Such an effort will not be easy at any level, given the deep resistance to change in schools (evident in the nationwide deep structure and in the state's tendency toward conservatism, paternalism, and hierarchical decision-making pattern).

Despite the state's long-standing resistance to change, the governor's excessively high profile, and the lack of a thoroughgoing dialogue, there is reason to hope. The involvement of political leaders is essential, and higher order learning is necessary if lasting reforms—and ones that are appropriate to the preparation of Arkansans for the increasingly information-centered world upon which they depend—are to be achieved and sustained. Given those essentials, one exceptionally promising policy direction would be not forcibly to consolidate but to support the small school and perhaps its urban counterpart, the "schools-within-a-school" plan. This reform would, however, be effective and lasting only if teachers and school boards are willing to undertake the promotion of higher order learning and be held accountable for it in ways mutually acceptable to the state and the particular community. Implementation of the small-school concept is recommended by the following factors: (1) the state's deep-structured tradition of small schools; (2) mounting research demonstrating that small schools manifest most of the crucial dimensions of effective schools, are well suited for the achievement of social and personal goals, and, given some outside resources, are also well suited for achieving the schools' intellectual goals;[27] (3) the unworkability of the top-down, regulatory, test-driven "first wave's" drive for "basics" and its accompanying bureaucratic, creativity-stifling, teacher-demoralizing results; and (4) the "second wave" agenda, with its restructuring experiments (one under the state education department and another under John Goodlad's Education Renewal Consortium). This next step, the support of small schools and the small-school concept, would have a greater chance to succeed than the current policies because it would combine the best of the past and the future, of traditional and modern Arkansas, perhaps even including the political leadership and ambition of its governor. It would be the best of the tradition of American federalism applied within Arkansas. For this policy direction to succeed there would, of course, have to be adjustments in the requirements and especially in the bureaucratic implementation of the "first wave." Each participating school would have to have a support plan that includes the utilization of such resources as higher education, a regional educational cooperative, and the private sector. It would not be easy and it would be long-term, but, as those who have systematically studied reform movements point out, sound, lasting reform *is* long-term.[28]

Finally, we return again to the original question, the subtitle of the chapter: "Can political leaders reform the schools?" The answer appears to be: "Not unless the leaders can provide and stimulate nurturing—as opposed to merely commanding—leadership, adjusting state mandates to the deep structure of schooling, the unique personality of each school, and the conditions of effective schools—particularly teacher efficacy and a clear mission shared by the entire staff and the school-community." In Arkansas, at least, reform will necessitate respecting the deep tradition of the small school, facilitating its support from federal, state, private sector, and higher education sources, supporting its unique personality and its sense of ownership, deciding its goals and long-term accountability procedures jointly, and helping its staff to stimulate new perspectives in imaginative ways to integrate the acquisition and uses of knowledge (i.e., higher *and* lower order learning). This proposal may reflect a distant ideal, but it is functional and one of the few answers that can do what all schools ought to be doing today: preparing youth for an information-centered and interdependent world, for civic responsibility, and for opening doors to the good life.

Curriculum Reform
& Professional Expertise:
The Florida Experience

C. J. B. MACMILLAN

In a 1984 report to the Florida Education Council, Marshall A. Harris of the Florida Department of Education listed 108 "reforms" that had taken place in Florida's education system up to that point of the Bob Graham governorship.

> Included are *new high school graduation requirements, longer high school days, merit pay for teachers and administrators, curriculum quality control, selection and compensation of school principals based on competence and performance, improved discipline, better textbook quality, school dropout prevention and reporting, greater emphasis on minority and disadvantaged students' needs, and more stimulating opportunities for high achieving students.*[1]

Included on the list are twenty reforms aimed at "expressing a higher regard for teachers," including such items as the merit-pay plan (since abolished), salary increases, the provision of workshops in specific areas (science and mathematics, especially), and experimental certification of arts and science graduates to teach in high schools. Also included are twenty-six items "providing quality assurance" and eight "making the academic experience more intense."[2]

In any reform movement, tensions exist between goals. When any one change is put into place, its success puts stress on other areas that are initially expected to continue unchanged; a change in graduation requirements, for example, will bring about changes in the teachers' tasks, for teachers will be the ones who have to provide additional instruction or spend more time on new subjects.

When more than one reform is proposed, the tensions are even greater. Such is the case in the educational reforms of recent years in Florida. As I will try to show in what follows, the legislature's attention to changing the curriculum of high schools—to "making the academic experience more intense" and to "providing quality assurance"—has an undesirable effect upon a concurrent worry, the development of an adequate teaching profession. Both are goals of the current reform movement, but the two goals may be unattainable when one is given precedence over the other.

We may assume that the development of competent professional teachers is a continuing goal in Florida's school reform movement; the development of "competency based" teacher education and evaluation through the 1970s is one indication of this goal, as are more recent attempts at increasing teacher salaries so as to attract more people to teaching. But the center of legislative and bureaucratic attention seems to have been on changes in the curriculum of all high schools in Florida. The effect of this approach upon the development of professional skills is the focus of this chapter.

In other words, what I shall focus upon is the implicit conflict between the goals (a) of providing "quality" academic education and (b) of "expressing a higher regard for teachers." The argument will proceed more as an analysis of trends than as an exposé of what has happened specifically.

Changing the Curriculum

Implicit in the school laws passed during the Graham era in Florida is one message: no student is to be educationally disadvantaged by the place where he or she lives. The assumption seems to have been that some districts (counties) presently have better schools than others, that a child would have a chance of receiving an inferior education by living in Alachua County, perhaps, as compared to Leon County. This is not something that a governor can live with comfortably, nor can the legislature. So in order to promote better education throughout the state—and thereby promote a better economic base for the state—several intertwining curricular measures have become law since about 1980.

For the most part, as might be expected, these new laws were the result of compromises between legislators, Department of Education specialists, and professional organizations. They are an attempt to provide for the protection of the public interest while preserving the rights of professional teachers and administrators. I shall first spell out a few of these changes and then return to what seems to me to be the dark side of this approach for teachers and teacher training.

A. Uniform requirements for graduation from high school were spelled out. In order to graduate from high school in Florida, as of the 1986–87 academic year, each student must have completed twenty-four academic credits (an academic credit is defined as 150 hours of instruction), distributed as follows:

1. Four credits in English, with major concentration in composition and literature
2. Three credits in mathematics
3. Three credits in science, two of which must have a laboratory component
4. One credit in American history
5. One credit in world history, including a comparative study of the history, doctrines, and objectives of all major political systems (This requirement takes the place of the Americanism vs. communism requirement of years before.)
6. One-half credit in economics, including a comparative study of the history, doctrines, and objectives of all major economic systems
7. One-half credit in American government
8. One-half credit in practical arts vocational education or exploratory vocational education
9. One-half credit in performing fine arts to be selected from music, dance, drama, painting, or sculpture

10. One-half credit in life-management skills to include consumer education, positive emotional development, nutrition, information and instruction on breast cancer detection and breast self-examination, cardiopulmonary resuscitation, drug education, and the hazards of smoking
11. One-half credit in physical education to include assessment, improvement, and maintenance of personal fitness
12. Nine elective credits.[3]

It should be noted that remedial courses may not be substituted for anything but elective credits; for example, students may not include a remedial writing or reading course among the English credits used for graduation. No more than nine elective remedial courses and no more than three credits in practical arts/home economics classes may be counted.

In addition, the law requires that each student have a 1.5 grade-point average in required courses and that each pass two examinations, the first showing "mastery of the minimum performance standards in reading, writing, and mathematics for the 11th grade" and the second demonstrating "ability to successfully apply basic skills to everyday life situations as measured by a functional literacy examination." These examinations are to be approved by the State Board of Education (i.e., the state cabinet).

Students who have attended high school and have taken the appropriate courses but who have not met the examination requirements "shall be awarded a certificate of completion" in a form to be determined by the state board. Local districts may have honors diplomas, if they so choose.

B. The State Board of Education has been directed to adopt "rules to provide for the development and periodic revision of uniform, statewide student performance standards, instruments, and assessment procedures to measure public-school-student performance in each major subject area or major area of study approved by the state board."[4] This was to have been done by the 1989–90 school year.

District school boards are directed to adopt student performance standards for each academic program for which credit toward high school graduation is awarded. Although "appropriate methods of assessing student mastery" are broad enough to include "teacher observations, classroom assignments, and examinations," the State Department of Education "shall review and make appropriate standards and policies adopted by the district."[5] They also have to provide technical assistance in the development of these standards and policies.

I take it that this directive means that each school district will have to try to meet state examination standards for each class taught in the schools. The emphasis is on the high schools, but it goes into the elementary and middle schools as well because of the uniform course framework policy.

The teeth of this law come with this provision: "Effective July 1, 1985, student performance standards must be incorporated in the pupil progression plan for students in grades 9 through 12 in order for the district to receive funding through the Florida Education Finance Program."[6] (The FEFP provides anywhere between 13 and 81 percent of local school budgets.)

C. The Department of Education (subject to State Board of Education review) is instructed to develop "curriculum frameworks" as well as student performance standards. Curriculum frameworks are discussed further:

The Department of Education shall develop, maintain, and revise as necessary curriculum frameworks for the purpose of ensuring instructional consistency and assessment within academic disciplines among public schools. A curriculum framework is a set of broad guidelines which aids educational personnel in producing specific instructional plans for a give subject area or area of study. The process for developing and periodically revising curriculum frameworks shall emphasize the recommendations of national professional organizations and instructional material consortia by subject area or area of study. The Department of Education shall develop, as part of the curriculum framework, intended outcomes specific to child abuse and neglect prevention and to drug and alcohol abuse prevention, which must be accomplished during the four progressional levels, K–3, 4–6, 7–9, and 10–12. Each such framework shall be initially approved by the State Board of Education by July 30, 1986.[7]

The student outcomes specified in these frameworks are to be the basis for the development of the "uniform, statewide student performance standards and assessment instruments."[8]

D. Florida has long been one of the twenty-three states that have a statewide adoption plan for instructional materials. This task is undertaken by "instructional materials councils" for each area and level of study on a six-year rotating basis. The councils are made up of four classroom teachers, two lay persons, one school board member, and two supervisors of teachers (i.e., the majority of members are "professionals"). The major task of these councils is now "to evaluate carefully all instructional materials submitted, to ascertain which instructional material, if any, submitted for consideration best implement those curricular objectives included within applicable curriculum frameworks approved by the State Board of Education and the state and district performance standards."[9] No limit was set for the number of texts or other materials that may go on the state list in any area of study; most seem to have ten to fifteen approved texts.

Within the Graham era, another feature of state adoption has developed, however. Worried about the quality of the texts available for use in the schools, Governor Graham urged that more attention be paid to the quality of the books. Accordingly, the legislature provided that pressure would be put upon local districts to use new texts as soon as possible after approval of new lists. Instead of using books until they are worn out, superintendents are now required to justify the use of old texts or texts not on the list.[10]

Discussion

As with any set of laws, this change in curriculum and student evaluation in the state has both good and bad features. My assessment of this change shall be based around one question:

What does it say about and to the individual teacher concerning his or her ability to make the decisions necessary in a professional context? My concern is for teacher autonomy and the development of professional expertise. The assumption is that to the extent that teachers are given a broad range of professional responsibility and many opportunities to exercise their expertise, they will be more competent than if they are expected merely to obey the commands of bureaucratic superiors.[11]

In a recent study, the Carnegie Foundation for the Advancement of Teaching found that 64 percent of Florida's teachers believed they were involved in choosing textbooks and instructional materials (only Maryland, where 61 percent believed themselves involved, was lower), and only 42 percent of Florida's teachers felt involved in shaping the curriculum (only Louisiana, where 40 percent felt involved, was lower). On other measures of teacher involvement (e.g., setting standards for student behavior, designing staff-development and in-service programs, deciding school budgets, and the selection of new teachers and administrators for the schools), Florida's teachers were below the national average.[12]

In his discussion of these findings, Ernest L. Boyer comments:

> Whatever is wrong with America's public schools cannot be fixed without the help of those inside the classroom. Yet in most states, teachers have been front-row spectators in a reform movement in which the signals are being called by governors, legislators, state education officials—those who are far removed from the field of action. . . .
>
> . . . If excellence is to be achieved and public confidence sustained, the local school must be answerable to the public for the performance of its students. But once again, it needs more freedom and more flexibility to do the job. In the end, American education must find a way to blend local control with national results.
>
> Above all, teachers must be full partners in the process. If we fail to give them more authority and a sense of their importance—as well as their responsibilities—we will have failed today's dedicated teachers and be unable to attract a new

generation of outstanding young people to serve in the classrooms of the nation. And by that failure, we will have limited tragically the educational possibilities of our children.[13]

One thing should stand out: The curriculum reforms in Florida reflect a lessening of local responsibility for establishing standards and curriculum. We all know that this is not a new thing; local control of schools has probably always been something of a myth, and anyone who would argue that local control is the rule in Florida has to face up to these laws as counterevidence.

Now, that's not all bad. At least it is recognized that Florida's schoolchildren are not going to be living in the backwoods all of their lives; the curriculum is justified as a necessity for living in the modern world. Leaving decisions about the curriculum in the hands of relatively unsophisticated local boards of education can have devastating effects, as witness the Columbia County (Lake City) Board of Education's recent removal of books containing the play *Lysistrata* and Chaucer's *Wife of Bath's Tale*. The anthology in which these were included was on the state-approved list of texts for humanities.

But what does it say about teachers? My assessment is this: In general, Florida's new curriculum laws reflect a distrust of individual teachers and of teachers as a group. This distrust devolves into a lessening of opportunity for teachers to make decisions that are part of what we mean by "professional competence." Let me weigh the evidence for this conclusion.

1. Begin with text selection. Although the majority of members of the state instructional materials councils are professional teachers, and although the advice of professional organizations is sought in the selection of texts, the fact of state selection—with ultimate approval of the texts in the hands of the elected state cabinet sitting as the board of education— assumes that decisions about instructional materials (and methods?) do not belong in the hands of those using the texts. This is a long-standing policy in the state of Florida and should be recognized as nothing new. What is new (i.e., within the present decade) is the requirement that the use of texts of other instructional materials from outside the list needs special jus-

tification. This requirement could go right down to the mimeographed materials a teacher might use to augment texts or published materials.

The Florida Board of Education has not been notable—as California's board has—for refusing texts because of their lack of quality; indeed, the most frequent reason for not approving texts seems to have been that the religious right objects to content or approaches exemplified in recent texts in social science or biology.

2. The use of statewide curriculum frameworks seems to assume that individual teachers—or even groups of teachers in local districts or schools—are not qualified to determine the content they are teaching, to organize courses, or to specify objectives, procedures, or even texts. It should be noted that one reason for developing statewide frameworks is to assure that the state-adopted list of texts will be appropriate to the state's curriculum. The requirement that the development of the frameworks be aided by consultation with professionals in the respective fields serves only to point up the fact that individual teachers are not given the responsibility for doing such things. It should not be forgotten that the final approval of the frameworks for individual courses is in the hands of the State Board of Education.

3. The use of statewide performance criteria, in turn, reflects this lack of respect for teachers. The determination of criteria for graduation from high school is not to be a decision of the profession but rather one to be made by professional politicians. Given the showing of the educational profession in the past, this may not be a bad thing; my assessment is that the profession has had a considerable part to play in the weakening of the schools in the last fifty years or so. And those who argue that educational decisions are at heart political could cheer at this acceptance of the fact. Political decisions, it might be held, should be in the hands of those who are elected to make hard political choices.

4. When all this is put into the context of an additional set of new laws—that is, those having to do with contracts, certification, and the necessity of annual evaluations carried out according to state-approved criteria—it is quite clear that the

teacher is being treated as one who is supposed to be responsive to the directives of those in the bureaucracy or political system rather than to criteria of professional expertise.[14] The teacher is an employee expected to carry out the will of the people or their political representatives, not to exemplify the best professional thinking.

For teachers, the bright side of this bureaucratization is that these state requirements could provide a buffer for individual teachers. If a teacher can show that he or she is following a state-mandated framework, using a state-approved text, there is less room for local critics to drive a political or religious wedge into the individual teacher's planning and practice. Granted, it provides an excuse for not being more creative or original; but it also provides a good barrier to political interference in the teacher's realm. The question is whether this apparent protection is worth the cost, especially when it seems relatively ineffective in the difficult cases. The Lake City prohibition of the humanities text and a recent brouhaha in Panama City over the use of books outside the list suggest that no amount of state buffering can protect professional creativity from the pressures toward uniformity.

Conclusions

The examination of a set of laws might not prove anything, for schools are remarkably conservative institutions in the face of new trends and fads. My discussion has proceeded on the prima facie assumption that the laws will be carried out and put into practice and that the tensions that are there in the laws will be felt in the classrooms of the state. The Carnegie Foundation's report supports this assumption—although it does not prove it. Does anything else need saying?

My prediction is that intellectually ambitious people who might go into teaching will seek elsewhere for occupations that will enable them to develop personally within a professional context. Those who do decide to fight it out are left in the position of having their professional skills and abilities downplayed, if they are even given a chance to develop.

Merit Pay: Resurrection of an Unworkable Past

KENNETH D. McCRACKEN &
DAVID J. VOLD

Following the lead of Governor Lamar Alexander and the state of Tennessee, merit pay has figured prominently in virtually all of the reform movements current in the southeastern states; it often stands out as the centerpiece of the school reform efforts. What's more, polls indicate public approval of merit pay by an almost two-to-one margin. Yet, despite the common acceptance of merit pay, one fact stands out: almost without exception, teachers oppose it.

It is awkward, to say the least, for teachers to admit to opposing merit pay. The principle of merit—"a person should get what he or she deserves" (or, "those who deserve more should get more")—sounds like simple justice. In fact, teachers do accept "merit" pay when it is awarded for additional work or for additional training (such a system has long been in place). Opposition arises when "merit" is determined by classroom performance. This was the key to Lamar Alexander's "Better Schools Program" and the main source of opposition by the Tennessee Education Association; it has made merit pay the teachers' bugaboo.

All distinctions aside, the public perception seems to be that, "like everybody else," teachers should be held accountable for what they do (or do not do). Because "what teachers do" is in the classroom, what better place to measure their worth? Merit pay not only rings true with the public's sense of fairness, it also appears to be consistent with common sense.

We are familiar with both merit and nonmerit systems in many walks of life other than teaching. Our experience has led us to the common sense that "justice works," that is, that the more closely income is tied to productivity, the greater productivity will be. So thoroughly is this notion believed that many would call it a natural law—the law of the marketplace. It lies at the root of the laissez-faire position: that government is best which governs least; that is, any interference with the law of the marketplace creates an artificial (hence unworkable) outcome. Those who hold to this view see it borne out in experience again and again.

There are many excellent examples of occupations that link income to productivity. Migrant farm laborers are paid according to the amount of produce they pick; salesmen are paid a commission reflecting the size of the sales they make; waitresses are paid (tips) corresponding to the cost of the meals they serve and the kind of service they provide. Merit systems are often employed in the fields of entertainment and athletics—of course, "merit" in these fields may be determined more by Nielsen ratings, or "drawing card" potential, than by talent or virtuosity, but pleasing the public is (arguably, at least) the object of these industries.

So often do we find the law of the marketplace borne out in our experience that we may imagine that it is universal. Yet, it is not. One notable exception arises when the state is the employer; then the law of the marketplace takes a back seat to the realities of politics. But must this be the case? Reformers, echoing Adam Smith, have long insisted that this cannot be the case—ultimately, the law of the marketplace must prevail.

Adam Smith embraced the principle of merit pay in 1776, when he reflected on the problem of motivation in *The Wealth of Nations*. There he divided occupations into two basic groups: productive and nonproductive (the latter of which teaching is a prime example—never mind the negative connotation attached to this term). Stated simply, Smith asked: Where there is no product, where is the motivation to produce? At a time when a professorship at a prestigious school was virtually a sinecure, Smith complained that professors at Oxford would not even go through the pretense of teaching after they had received their tenure. Smith expended considerable effort in trying to develop a system in which teachers would be rewarded for their diligence.

The key to motivating productivity in a "nonproductive" occupation is to find a hidden (or substitute) product. Supposedly, the "nonproductive" worker will realize a "nonproductive" (i.e., unmeasurable) goal *at the same time* that the "productive" (i.e., measurable) tasks are fulfilled. For the attorney (whose nonproductive goal is justice), the productive goal might mean winning cases—the more victories, the better the attorney is said to be (and, supposedly, the better justice is served). For the physician (whose nonproductive goal is health), the productive goal might entail seeing more patients and receiving high fees—the wealthier the physician, the more successful we may judge him or her to be (i.e., in the primary task of promoting health).

If the success of the (nonproductive) attorney can be determined by comparing a cases-won/cases-lost record and the success of the (nonproductive) physician can be determined by measuring a patient-load/fee-structure record, why couldn't a measure be found for determining the success of the (nonproductive) teacher? Why couldn't the outcome of an education be quantified and recorded on a standardized test? Then the success or failure of a teacher could be said to correspond to the rate at which the teacher's students did well or did poorly on that standardized test. What's more, teachers would be motivated to succeed if their pay were tied to their students' success on the test.

Yet, as motivating as "merit" pay is, might it not have some dangers? We can understand what may happen when an IRS bureaucrat's salary is contingent on the amount of money he or she collects in taxes or when a police officer's salary is contingent on the number of traffic tickets he or she issues. We know that farm workers, who are paid by the volume of fruits or vegetables picked, may pick produce that is too ripe or not ripe enough or may even include rocks or dirt with the produce in order to increase their pay. We do not regard caveat emptor as a badge of pride worn by the commission salesman. We are dismayed by the impact of the profit motive on the integrity of the physician and the attorney. There is no doubt that "merit" pay motivates greater productivity of some sort; the problem is, it may be the wrong sort—it may even include lying, cheating, and stealing.

There may be some objection to linking "merit" with high-pressure salesmanship or morally reprehensible acts. After all, "merit" connotes something positive, more akin to "earn" and "deserve." Therein lies the problem. Merit pay always sounds right—that's why it typically is popular with everyone except those upon whom it is applied. It is of the nature of a tautology: "Those who deserve more should get more." While it may sound reasonable, it is not. "Deserve" means "should get." The principle of merit turns out to say: "Those who should get more should get more." What it does not establish is that *anyone* should get more.

Of course, those who deserve more deserve more, but who is it (and on what grounds?) that deserves more? Because the tautological nature of the merit-pay principle goes unnoticed, reformers are too eager to apply it, to bypass the philosophical spadework inherent in coming to grips with what it would mean to deserve more and to adopt a merit-pay plan. The end result is that criteria by which merit can be measured are manufactured. This is not a problem unique to education; and wherever it occurs, it always leads to trouble.

The operational "merit" of a bureaucratic manager is often based on the simple criterion of the number of persons working within that particular unit. The motivation in this instance is obvious. If the manager can create more work, he or she can claim the necessity of hiring more workers. If more workers can be hired, the manager may "deserve" a promotion. This spiral of inefficiency has led to several interesting attempts at making bureaucracies more responsive, less governed by artificial criteria.

A model of merit used for this purpose, and utilized by the University of Tennessee, is based on the book *The Practice of Management,* by Peter Drucker.[1] Drucker presents a method for "unboxing" administrators, especially those at higher levels. His fundamental premise is that jobs should be fitted to personalities rather than personalities fitted to jobs. Drucker's method of evaluation critiqued the objectives of given positions as much as the given individuals in those positions. This method of evaluation is similar to a plan of evaluation that was in vogue during the 1950s and 1960s in which schools were evaluated for the purpose of improving instruction. Indeed, such a method of evaluation has been suggested in a paper developed by no fewer than four major education organizations: the American Association of School Administrators, the National Association of Elementary School Principals, the National Association of Secondary School Principals, and the National Education Association.[2]

Drucker's conclusions derive from his study of the characteristics of professionals in business organizations. He observed that professionals want to make a contribution to their organization as well as to know that they are making one. In addition to making a contribution, professionals also want to be recognized by other members of their profession (i.e., beyond the confines of their particular business); this desire may be in conflict with the interests of their employers, whose focus is more restricted to the business. Unfortunately, while Drucker's recommendations for promotions and financial incentives for increased performance have received a great deal of attention, his recommendation concerning the professional wishes of employees have often been ignored.[3]

Teachers have had only minimal opportunities for recognition by their peers; however, even these opportunities may be in jeopardy if merit systems are adopted. Most merit systems offer little to reward those who have achieved recognition by other teachers in other parts of the country. Instead, the typical merit system restricts the opportunity for professional recognition. Merit systems are seldom developed in such a manner as to enhance a teacher's reputation elsewhere. Merit systems are built to enhance the status of the local school and to reward the teacher's contributions to the school.

The history of merit systems demonstrates, moreover, that

they have never been developed by the individuals who are subject to them. The wisdom of such mechanisms is questionable. It is very doubtful that those who lack input into an organization's decision making (as opposed to implementing the decisions of others) would be willing to ally themselves with the goals of that organization. As a way of counteracting this alienation from the organization, some school administrators have made the point of *telling* teachers how important they are in the process. However, words that are not backed up by genuine teacher involvement are more likely to create a credibility gap than a sense of loyalty and involvement.

Professional prestige is also developed through association with universities—a cardinal criterion for status in any profession is an advanced degree. University association is very strongly related to recognition by other professionals in one's academic specialty.

Certain occupations have been struggling for decades to achieve professional status. Nursing is a prime example, as is teaching. However, the current reform measures threaten the advances teachers have made in this regard. While the reforms do not do away with degree requirements, they lessen their importance. For example, the Tennessee Better Schools Program explicitly states that performance in the classroom takes precedence over the degree.[4]

While it could be argued that performance is a better criterion for judgment than is a degree, this has not been the pattern used by the classical professions (law, medicine, and theology) in establishing professional status. There (aside from a few denominations that affect some ministers), one can do nothing without the appropriate advanced degree. Such requirements imply that the attainment of the degree is the first criterion for acceptance into the profession. Naturally, such standards create a strong connection between the university and professional fields as a whole.

By emphasizing techniques and skills over degree, the reform proposals reduce teaching to the level of a craft, a return to the view of teaching current in the early parts of this century (it is interesting that William C. Bagley, writing in 1908, used the term "school-craft" when he referred to skills of teaching).[5] Merit systems tend to be based on the assumption that teaching is little more than a skill that can be learned by supervised repetition.

Merit systems are probably a part of a larger movement that is characteristic of the 1980s. The latter seems to be a reaction to the 1960s, which may have been a reaction to the 1950s. The 1980s have seen the revival of "horse-and-buggy" concepts, unaccompanied by the horse and buggy. The decade has been characterized by a type of nostalgia satirized by Will Rogers when he said, "It's not like it was in the good old days; and it never was."

During the past decade, it has become fashionable to condemn public school teachers and public schools, with President Reagan taking the lead and Secretary of Education Bennett joining in. None of Reagan's proposals reflected the spirit of public education, and Bennett made a point of endorsing private schooling. In Tennessee, Governor Alexander never seemed to find anything to praise in the public schools or the teachers of Tennessee except as they responded to his call. More extreme conservatives have called for the virtual end of public education.

What's more, the 1980s seem to have been marked by a resurgence of essentialism and its attendant practices: accountability, behavioral objectives, management by objectives, programmed instruction, and "back to basics." On the decline are such values as adaptability, critical thinking, the learning of principles over the learning of facts, bringing out the abilities of children, and development of subject matter from the learner's point of view.

It will require some courage to go against the current, to abandon criteria that lend themselves to easy measurement within the limits of our technology. But our need is not for measurement, it is for conversation. We have too many questions— many of them not yet addressed. We also have lessons, *learned but not applied.*

If merit pay is the march of the future, we can start on the right foot by giving teachers the primary responsibility for determining the criteria by which merit will be measured. If merit pay is going to succeed, the system must establish and enhance the recipients' reputations among other teachers beyond the schools or school districts where they work. Furthermore, merit pay should not be introduced unless and until the salary base is substantially increased for all teachers. Otherwise, those who do not get merit pay will perceive that they are financing the higher salaries of those who do, causing resentment and undermining the whole educational enterprise. Finally, merit needs to be tied to university degrees, but the degrees should do more than reflect the mastery of a teaching skill. The emphasis ought to be on the teacher's professional understanding, especially on such theoretical disciplines as history of education and philosophy of education.

Before we introduce another flawed reform, we need to ask where we want it to take us. Would it be enough if American students were outperforming Japanese students on mathematics exams? What is important? What does it mean to be educated?

Part Two

Educational Reform in Mississippi: A Historical Perspective

ROBERT L. JENKINS &
WILLIAM A. PERSON

The development of public education in Mississippi, while not unique among southern states, nevertheless represents something of an extreme case. A dominant contributing factor in this development has been the lack of commitment by state leaders to fund state-supported schools adequately. This lack of commitment, however, is not obvious from a review of the state's historical educational documents. Rhetorical support for public education by state leaders, especially among governors, has been clear and positive.

Mississippi's historical documents concerning education are replete with perennial questions such as: Who shall be educated? How shall they be educated? For how long shall they be educated? How shall their education be financed? Who shall provide their educational experiences? What types of educational experiences shall be provided? Indeed, many of the concerns addressed in the Mississippi Education Reform Act of 1982 can be traced back through the state's educational history. Among the specific concerns related to Mississippi's public education development are: funding, school district organization, teacher pay, teacher preparation, compulsory school attendance, uniformity of school provisions in the state code, and the adequacy of preparation of students who have completed their education in the state's public schools.

In this chapter, it is our intent to provide: (1) a brief historical overview of education in Mississippi, (2) a general description of the Mississippi Education Reform Act of 1982, and (3) an analysis of the educational impact stemming from that act.

Antebellum Legislation

Perhaps the most significant educational legislation in Mississippi prior to the Civil War was enacted in 1846 during the administration of Governor Albert Gallatin Brown, a strong proponent of a statewide system of common schools. This statute, which provided for a uniform and general system of common schools, is described in this way by historian Mary F. Sumners:

> Under this law the board of county commissioners was empowered to license teachers and disburse county school funds. Each county was permitted to levy taxes for support of its common schools. Many counties, however, refused to establish school systems under this general law, and it was eventually repealed. Thereafter, special statutes were enacted authorizing common schools in particular counties desiring them.[1]

The 1846 statute included the requirement that the written consent of the majority of heads of families in each township be secured before taxes could be levied. Apparently, such consent was difficult to obtain. Still, according to historian William D. McCain, approximately 125 special statutes authorizing common schools were enacted for the benefit of townships, counties, groups of counties, and municipalities between 1848 and 1860.[2] Without a doubt, the prevailing attitude (at least by those who were in power) during this period was that education should be strictly controlled at the local level and that state laws should serve to accommodate the specific whims and conditions of the various local governments throughout the state. Consequently, public schools lacked any semblance of uniformity.

Post–Civil War Legislation (1868–1930)

The Civil War took precedence over everything else in the minds of the Mississippi leadership. Hence, little attention was given to education then. Shortly after the war, during the so-called Reconstruction years, attention was once again directed toward establishing a uniform system of common schools. For instance, the newly organized State Teachers Association passed a resolution in January 1867 calling for a public school system:

> Resolved, 1. That the enactment of a public school system that shall meet the wants and necessities of the entire population is desideratum of the utmost importance.
> 2. That it is the duty as well as the interest of the state, through its legislature, to establish and maintain normal schools in different parts of the state for the purpose of educating colored teachers, so that they may be qualified to labor as teachers among the colored population of the state.
> 3. That it would be for the interest of the people and the promotion of education to have a uniform system.[3]

A year later, in 1868, a constitutional convention, referred to by historians as the Black and Tan Convention because it consisted primarily of northern white Republicans and former slaves, drafted the state's third constitution.[4] The first attempt to ratify this constitution failed in June 1868, due to a disenfranchisement provision affecting a large number of former Confederates. It was ratified in December 1869, however, when the disenfranchisement provision was deleted, and it was signed into law in 1870 by Governor James L. Alcorn.[5]

The new constitution provided: (1) that all children between the ages of five and twenty-one years have equal advantages in the public schools; (2) that a State Department of Education, a State Superintendent of Education, and a State Board of Education (consisting of the state superintendent, the secretary of state, and the state attorney general) be established; (3) that there be free public schools in each county that constituted a district (except in those counties with a population of 3,000 or more in incorporated municipalities, which organized as separate school districts); (4) that county superintendents and boards of school directors perform specified duties; and (5) that the responsibility of the board of supervisors to levy a special school tax not exceed fifteen mills.[6]

In 1890, Mississippi adopted its fourth (and present) state constitution. Few changes were made concerning the operation of the schools. In one respect, the system of public schools was strengthened by a provision specifying a minimum four-month term. Local school districts had the option of operating longer terms if they were willing to tax themselves to do so. Most notable, however, was the provision mandating separate schools for black and white children.[7] While this practice was fixed in Mississippi by 1890, the constitutional provision gave it the sanction of law. Six years later, legal sanction of racial segregation on a national basis was provided by the United States Supreme Court in the case of *Plessy v. Ferguson,* which established the "separate but equal" doctrine.

In 1896, the Mississippi legislature created a State Board of Examiners for the purpose of issuing state licenses to teachers. Prior to this legislation, the responsibility for certifying teachers was that of the state superintendent, who delegated authority to a county examining board (consisting of the county superintendent and two teachers or college graduates).[8] The state licenses granted by the State Board of Examiners were good for one to three years, depending upon how well the applicant performed on the examination. After receiving a state license for a second time, a teacher was exempted from any further examination.[9]

Between 1900 and 1930, the primary educational concerns in Mississippi centered on the creation of a textbook commission, improved funding, and compulsory school attendance. In 1904, the legislature passed a uniform textbook law upon the recommendation of Governor James K. Vardaman, one of the South's most notable Progressive Era governors. This law authorized the governor to name an eight-member textbook commission, consisting of public school teachers and the state superintendent (in an ex officio capacity), to select textbooks to be used in all public schools for five years. The law established that textbooks were to be adopted in the following subjects: civic government, composition, elements of agriculture, English grammar, geography, history of Mississippi, intellectual arithmetic, orthography, physiology, practical arithmetic, reading, United States history, and writing.[10]

When Henry L. Whitfield became state school superintendent in 1898, he had been quite concerned with the poor condition of school buildings, especially in the rural areas of the
state. Consequently, he undertook an extensive building program—particularly for the building of new schools for white,
rural students. Later (around 1920), new school buildings were
also constructed for black students through matching grants
from the Julius Rosenwald Fund. Additionally, during this period approximately fifty agricultural high schools were established.[11] Of course, this effort was directly responsive to the
dominant agrarian economy of the state.

Another effort directly related to the state's agricultural
economy was the legislature's almost immediate vote to accept
funds created by the Smith-Hughes Act of 1917. This act
provided federal matching support for agricultural and home
economics curricular experiences at the high school level.

The legislature also addressed other means of improving education. According to Jim B. Pearson and Edgar Fuller, the legislature

> authorized graduates of the University of Mississippi and other
> colleges to receive professional licenses when they had taken
> sufficient professional courses, improved the consolidation laws,
> fixed the salaries of the county superintendents and required
> them to have more training and increased the common school
> appropriations. At the same time, the General Education Board,
> the Julius Rosenwald Fund, the [Anna] Jeanes Fund, and the
> Slater Fund continued contributing to Negro education, includ-
> ing money for new schoolhouses and for paying teachers to su-
> pervise in the Negro elementary schools.[12]

The final major piece of legislation considered during this
period was the compulsory school attendance law. Mississippi
was the last state in the nation to pass a compulsory school
attendance law, in 1918. Perhaps, as Kern Alexander and Kenneth Forbis Jordan point out, because Mississippi was largely
"an immobile society oriented to an agrarian and appren-
ticeship economy, the need for compulsory education was not
perceived to be as great as in a mobile industrialized society."[13]
It is estimated that 90 percent of the population either was di-

rectly involved in agriculture or was in industries related to or dependent upon agriculture.[14]

The racial issue also influenced Mississippi's failure to enact a compulsory school attendance law. Newspapers of this period are replete with expressions of white concerns about the implications of such a statute. Fearful that compulsory public education might threaten the segregated status quo, white Mississippians were reluctant to accept the legal practice of required school attendance.[15]

Two factors probably contributed to Mississippi's finally enacting a compulsory attendance law. First, Mississippi was under considerable pressure to pass such a law because it was the only state in the nation that had not done so by 1915. Second, the concern expressed by many educational leaders about the high rate of illiteracy in the South brought unquestionable attention to the state of Mississippi. A case in point is William H. Hand's study, *The Need of Compulsory Education in the South,* which concluded: "Compulsory education reduces illiteracy and the South sorely needs to have hers reduced."[16] Without a doubt, this charge was applicable to the state of Mississippi.

It could be argued that the initial compulsory school attendance law in Mississippi (House Bill No. 143) was largely symbolic. Although it required children between the ages of seven and fourteen years to attend school at least sixty days per school year, it allowed the local boards of education to reduce that number to forty days. Fines of no less than one dollar but no more than ten dollars could be levied by the county superintendent against parents for noncompliance. However, the compulsory attendance law could only be enforced if 20 percent of the qualified voters in any county petitioned the board of supervisors for a vote on the matter and, subsequently, a majority voted in favor of the law in a special election. A county that did not want compulsory attendance need do nothing, as the petition and special election were not mandatory.[17]

The first enforceable compulsory school attendance law was not passed until 1920. This law (House Bill No. 177) required at least eighty days of school attendance, which could not be reduced by the local school board. It was still possible for a county to avoid compulsory attendance, but House Bill No. 177

required a petition and special election to nullify it. This vote-out provision (rather than the vote-in provision of the initial law) made it difficult for counties to ignore the intention of the law. In fact only four of Mississippi's eighty-two counties voted the law out.[18]

Despite the political rhetoric of Governor James K. Vardaman to abolish public education for black students during this period, the passage of an enforceable compulsory school attendance law (at least in part) brought a dramatic increase in public school enrollment during the 1920s.[19] According to State Superintendent W. F. Bond, over 60,000 more children were in school in 1921 than had been there before 1920. By 1925, this number was reported to be over 100,000.[20]

Post-Depression Legislation (1934–1982)

Just as Mississippi was beginning to experience a positive impact from its enforceable compulsory school attendance law, the Great Depression created a chaotic economic situation for the state's public schools. In part, that situation was mitigated, in 1932, when a retail sales tax was enacted and signed into law, enabling the public schools to regain and maintain a better financial condition. Yet, even with this new law and federal funds of over $1.3 million during the 1933–35 period, teachers and bus drivers were due $1 million in back pay by 1935.[21]

An important step toward financial stability was taken with the passage of the Kyle-Cook Budget Law of 1936. Basically, this law required local superintendents to submit estimated expenditures for the support, maintenance, and operation of their schools each year. Not surprisingly, the new budget process resulted in dramatic improvements in the educational accounting procedures at both the local and the state levels.

Another important development occurred in 1940, when the legislature passed a bill creating the Mississippi State Textbook Purchasing Board. In addition to outlining the membership and selection process for the board, the law stipulated the power, duties, and penalties for violation of the newly established free textbook adoption procedures.[22]

Mississippians had to wait thirteen years for the next major school-related legislation: the creation of a six-member Educational Finance Commission in 1953. The commission's charge was to reorganize school districts and to allocate appropriated funds for the construction of school facilities. In order to assure that the commission could carry out its charge, the legislature abolished all existing school districts. Eventually, the commission reorganized the state into 151 school districts.[23]

Following the reorganization legislation, attention shifted to a highly controversial topic: school desegregation. The United States Supreme Court decreed in the 1954 case of *Brown v. Board of Education of Topeka (Kansas)* that de jure segregation was no longer constitutional. In reaction, Mississippi passed a constitutional amendment authorizing the Mississippi legislature to abolish public education if it was deemed necessary to preserve segregation. In 1956, the legislature exercised its authority and repealed the compulsory school attendance law.

State Superintendent J. M. Tubb opposed the repeal of the compulsory school attendance law and continued to search for ways to have it reinstated. Unable to produce convincing dropout statistics to support his position, Tubb made a final appeal to the legislature in his last biennial report:

> We expressed a belief in our first Report that our compulsory school law needed strengthening. It was repealed by the Legislature in 1956. During the past decade Mississippi has had no such law. The Legislature in 1968 can do well by our people by re-enacting a law that will have compelling power. The law that was repealed in 1956 was a weak law; it needed strengthening then, and even more now. When Mississippi adopted a compulsory school law in the beginning it was the last state in the Union to do so, and now again Mississippi stands alone in this respect. We recommend that such a law be re-enacted and strengthened in its re-enactment.[24]

In 1973 Governor William Waller authorized the establishment of a Public Education Study Committee to undertake a comprehensive study and evaluation of the state's role in public schools. Chaired by Senator Sam Wright, the committee's recommendations addressed such areas as school attendance counseling, early childhood education, district reorganization, accountability, more equitable methods of financing schools, the need for an expanded state board of education, and teacher dismissal procedures. Significantly, it included no consideration of increasing teacher salaries.[25]

In 1977 the legislature acted upon one of the recommendations of the Public Education Study Committee, passing a comprehensive attendance counseling program. The intent of this legislation was to encourage school attendance of children between the ages of seven and thirteen years but not to compel them to do so; noncompliance brought neither fines nor penalties.

Still, it appears that the state leadership had come to the realization, as early as the mid-1960s, that significant progress could not take place without an educated citizenry. A case in point was Senate Bill No. 1670, authorizing the Mississippi Research and Development Council to contract for an exhaustive study of the state's educational needs and "to make recommendations calculated to produce a coordinated educational program which will attain the maximum development of human and other resources of the state."[26] Another example was Governor Paul B. Johnson's letter of transmittal to fellow Mississippians, highlighting two of the major concerns of the report. He declared: "(1) our children are not receiving as effective an education as they need, if they are to compete successfully in the world in which they are going to have to make a living; and (2) our economic development goals cannot be achieved unless we greatly strengthen our total educational system."[27]

It seems clear that, by the mid-1960s, both the state legislative and the executive leadership recognized what needed to be done to realize significant economic development. The major question that remained was how best to achieve an effective educational program for the state's more than one-half million school-age children. Subsequent study committees (such as the Public Education Study Committee), legislative action, and executive leadership at the state superintendent's level continued to address the question of how to achieve an effective system of public education. As the decade of the 1970s came to a close, all that remained was for legislators to feel a groundswell for education emanating from the people in the small towns and rural areas of the state.

The Mississippi Education Reform Act of 1982: Antecedents

Mississippians of a century ago may well have recited a variety of responses had they been asked: "What ills most retard the state's development?" Almost assuredly one answer would have cited the state's poor economic conditions. Primarily rural and agricultural, Mississippi was wedded to a cotton-tenancy system that trapped most of its people in chronic poverty. Its effects were telling and visible everywhere.

Economically, the state is quite different today. No longer dependent on one-crop agriculture, Mississippi has moved dramatically in diversifying its economy. For nearly two decades now, manufacturing has occupied the central place in the economy, serving as the major employer and income producer for working-class Mississippians.[28]

Despite such changes, however, poverty remains endemic in the Mississippi population. Occupying a position relatively unchanged during the twentieth century, Mississippi's per capita income level is the lowest in the nation. And each year the gap between Mississippi and its sister states grows larger. Transfer payments through social security and federal and state welfare provide the greatest source of income for citizens in fifty-one of the state's eighty-two counties. High rates of unemployment are a persistent problem in the industrial sector's numerous light-manufacturing jobs.[29] By most statistical accounts, Mississippi is the poorest state in the Union. Hence, most citizens today would probably give the same response to the above question as their counterparts of several generations ago.

Few informed Mississippians would also fail to classify the state's poor educational system as one of the greatest impediments to state progress. Indeed, just as economic data have reminded them of their general impoverishment, grim statistics have substantiated Mississippi's poor record and lowly status in educating its citizenry. In virtually every category of public education, from high school graduation rates and expenditures per schoolchild to pupil performance on standardized tests or teacher salaries, statistics have regularly placed Mississippi at or near the bottom of the nation.

Such statistics have led the state to a sobering reassessment of its priorities. In recent years, citizens have come to a greater understanding of the relationship between economic impoverishment and a poor educational system. Perhaps at no time in the state's history has this relationship been more skillfully communicated than in the successful 1979 gubernatorial campaign of William Winter.

Like many of his predecessors, Winter campaigned on a platform of raising Mississippi from the nation's economic cellar. This could be done, he contended, by attracting jobs to the state. However, creating new jobs required that the state first address its poor climate of public education. Mississippi's people simply lacked the necessary skills to appeal to the more profitable manufacturing and service industries. If elected, Winter promised to make public school improvement one of his administration's top priorities.[30]

Winter's campaign promises were more than rhetoric. For two years following his election, he proposed a package of education improvements that included compulsory attendance laws, higher teacher pay, statewide kindergartens, improved vocational and technical training, and the creation of a trust fund to underwrite educational and economic development. The legislature remained unmoved. Some lawmakers were sensitive to the needed improvements but were held back by their concerns over the state's poor financial situation. Winter's proposals were expensive—kindergartens alone were estimated to cost more than $30 million.[31] Legislators were simply unwilling to take the political risk of imposing new taxes on the citizens. "Right now people are anti-new tax. Next year is election time, and taxes aren't popular in elections," commented one of the legislature's most powerful leaders.[32]

The governor remained determined. Mississippi could act decisively now by paying the needed cost to educate its young and make them "self-sufficient, productive and able to qualify for the good jobs," he said, or it would have to pay a toll "in terms or welfare . . . [and other] social costs down the road."[33] Unable to move the legislature from its obstinacy, Winter took his case directly to the people.

Winter established a grassroots campaign to promote education reform. He enlisted the help of leading citizens, public leaders, and public and professional groups who supported his educational ideas. Vowing to work to defeat legislators who refused to respond to the needed changes, during the summer and fall of 1982 these educational recruits helped mobilize the state in support of Winter's education forums.[34]

The education forums were held in nine cities across the state to generate support for Winter's plan for a special legislative session to pass a comprehensive package of education reforms. The forums attracted large numbers of interested voters who overwhelmingly approved the governor's stand. "I don't think you can have meetings like he's had and not have some impact on the Legislature," commented one lawmaker after a meeting attended by more than 1,200 people in a driving rainstorm.[35] The citizens of the state sent a clear message to the legislature and few failed to recognize it.

Winter's accurate reading of the popular will culminated in a special legislative session in December 1982. Utilizing a special educational study prepared by an out-of-state consulting firm, Winter proposed a package of innovative and practical changes "essential for this state to have a competitive system of education." The estimated cost was $65 million.[36] Although the governor did not get his entire package, the legislature, after two weeks in special session, passed House Bill No. 4, the Mississippi Education Reform Act of 1982.

The Education Reform Act was one of the most far-reaching pieces of legislation in the state's history. It catapulted the state into the forefront of educational reform some time before such reform became a national trend. And it served as a model for other states. Most important of all, it held the promise for correcting some of the state's most pressing problems. Predictions were abundant about the potential of the act "to turn education around in Mississippi" and move the state progressively forward.[37]

The Education Reform Act was, indeed, comprehensive. Containing some forty-eight sections, the act was designed to strengthen the role of educational leadership at the state level, improve pupil achievement, increase teacher and administrator competencies, reward the demonstrated ability of school personnel, and increase accountability procedures at all levels in the public educational process. Funding for most of the new and innovative measures was designated to come from increased sales and use taxes as well as increases in corporate and individual income taxes.

The Mississippi Education Reform Act:
Description and Analysis

Since the passage of the Education Reform Act, much has been said about its merits and potential for positive educational gains. But what has its impact really been? How have citizens reacted to the law and its implications for immediate and future changes in their communities? Has the act, as supporters envisioned, facilitated an educational climate conducive for significant economic benefits to occur? In this section, these fundamental questions are addressed. The concerns here are with the key sections of the law, particularly those that are readily identified as major departures from Mississippi's educational past and that represent significant and innovative advances in Mississippi's educational experience.

Although most of the act remains in place, several features have undergone significant modification. Influenced by a number of factors, including the feasibility and practicality of implementation and especially the realities of local and state politics, some measures have been totally discarded. Nowhere was this modification more obvious than in the case of the provision mandating reorganization of the state's numerous school districts.

Not since the early 1950s had Mississippi made a realistic effort to address the need of school reorganization. In 1953 the state underwent a massive program of reorganizing the many one-room schoolhouses and reducing the 3,952 school districts to a more manageable 151. Clearly, reducing the number of schools, and the districts under which they functioned, represented a move into a more modern era of school governance. Generally, the action provided for more efficiently operated schools as well as greater opportunity for the state's schoolchildren to enlarge their educational experience through the benefits of a wider range of curriculum offerings.[38]

But many problems persisted. Even maintaining 151 districts in a state suffering from limited financial resources burdened the educational system. Many small and poor districts, having to contend with small local tax bases, were already strained in providing their students with the minimum curriculum offerings necessary to meet state standards and allow them to enter higher education. The Education Reform Act, with its new accreditation measures requiring a new standard statewide curriculum, meant that many of these same districts would have to add new courses, creating an even greater hardship on them. Complications arose too because of the lack of any uniformity of governance in the various types of school systems in existence across the state. Hence, conventional wisdom dictated that the Education Reform Act address the question of school district reorganization.

Opposition to school reorganization arose immediately. Community ties to schools are deeply rooted, especially among citizens of small rural communities where reorganization could spell the greatest changes. The prospect of losing their schools and transporting their children across county lines into another district was, for many, "almost unthinkable." A parent speaking against reorganization at a local meeting conducted by the Educational Finance Commission expressed the sentiments not only of her community but of small communities across the state when she said, "We don't intend to give up without a fight."[39] But even among more affluent and efficient school districts, reorganization was seldom regarded as an appealing solution to one of the state's most pressing educational problems. In most cases, it meant assuming additional responsiblities and financial burdens that citizens were not very willing to accept.

State political leaders had little trouble in supporting their constituents against school district reorganization. For many of them, reorganization had been the least acceptable provision of the Education Reform Act anyway. These legislators had opposed including the measure in the act but were effectively thwarted by legislative negotiators. Reorganization champions had skillfully injected the plan into the compromise version of the act so that "lawmakers were forced to accept or reject the entire package without having an opportunity to consider reorganization as a separate issue."[40] The problem, remarked one key senate opponent of reorganization, was that the Education Reform Act's "track was greased so good, and the train was moving so fast" that it was impossible to exclude reorganization from the law.[41]

For both political and personal reasons, legislators became some of the most outspoken critics of reorganization. "You talk about closing schools, that's like lynching your grandmother," commented one lawmaker representing a rural senate district.[42] Despite the pleas of reorganization advocates, who stressed the importance of "adequacy and equity"in the state's schools, reorganization seemed doomed from the outset, and in 1985 the state legislature repealed this section from the law.[43]

Although the Education Reform Act made no specific reference to district governance, it was implied in the charge to the Educational Finance Commission to assess the efficiency of local school operations.[44] Educational leaders could point to several inadequacies in Mississippi's schools directly attributable to a lack of uniformity in education laws. Specifically, reformers sought to bring about greater uniformity in school district organization, the funding process, and the method of selecting district superintendents.

Under existing state law, four major school organizational arrangements are permissible. Different in structure from each other, the organizational patterns include county districts (which embrace schools in all of the territory of a county, except territory in a municipal separate and consolidated district), consolidated districts (which include districts other than county or municipal separate districts), municipal separate districts (embracing schools within corporate limits of a municipality), and special municipal separate districts (existing when an area added to a municipal separate district contains 25 percent or more of a county's educable children).[45] Each school district is governed by a board of trustees, membership of which is determined by election, appointment, or a combination of both. All districts are administered by a superintendent, elected in all county districts but selected by the board of trustees in the other districts. In all districts, except the municipal separate ones, the county board of supervisors maintains budgetary and taxing authority for the schools.[46]

Differences in district organizational structures have frequently complicated efforts made by educational leaders and reformers to improve education in the state. The fact that most districts lacked fiscal independence has been especially critical in limiting funding increases for school support. Such districts were required to pass their school budgets and then wait for what was often an extended period of time to see if county boards of supervisors would fund them. Frequently, the result was underfunding because of county officials' unwillingness to raise taxes or to shift monies from other areas to support expanding educational needs. For many years, only municipal separate districts were authorized to increase school taxes. Such increases were limited to no more than 10 percent of the previous year's budget, but largely because of this power municipal separate districts have been generally regarded as the most effective school districts in the state. Because of the effectiveness of the municipal separate districts, educational leaders have pressed for similarly organized districts on a statewide basis.[47] To some extent, progress has been made in this area. Recent enabling legislation permits county school districts to increase their budgets to no more than 7 percent over the previous year.[48] Changes such as these have facilitated the expansion of district fiscal independence but have not eliminated confusion and some expenses resulting from the lack of uniformity under current district organization structures.[49]

Advocates of uniform school laws have also questioned the practice of electing county district superintendents. While the competency of these officials is no longer a major issue, educational leaders have been concerned over the continuous need for elected superintendents to be politically active. If they hope to hold their offices very long it is necessary to "be a politician first and effective administrator second."[50] Supporters of change argue that appointing county superintendents would eliminate this problem. Moreover, they claim such a method would "bring more professionalism" to county districts by allowing the district boards to pick the best qualified leaders from a significant pool of applicants. Finally, studies have suggested that student performance on achievement tests is affected both by district organization and by the method of selecting school superintendents; when both factors of budget-making independence and appointed superintendent are present, students have generally performed better on achievement tests.[51]

In November 1984 the Educational Finance Commission approved changes designed to provide for a more uniform set of school laws. Like the reorganization issue, however, the proposed changes quickly drew opposition. Indeed, opponents of reorganization, recently victorious in their fight against the Educational Finance Commission's reorganization initiatives, regarded the uniform law proposals as merely "a backdoor approach" to school district reorganization.[52] County supervisors, threatened with the loss of important budgetary and taxing power, and elected superintendents voiced the loudest opposition. They were soon joined by legislators, some of whom were troubled by what appeared to be an assumption of excessive power by the Educational Finance Commission. Changes along the lines recommended by the commission were not authorized by the Education Reform Act's reorganization provision, noted a legislator known for his support of education, but were "left with the Legislature, and we have not decided."[53]

When the legislature did decide, it was not in favor of the commission's recommendations. For both personal and political reasons, legislators, particularly those from small rural school districts, refused to make any concessions that would lead to elimination of their school districts. Educational leaders have continued to lobby for effective change in the state's district governance laws, but there appears to be little sentiment either from the citizens of the state to press for uniform education laws or from the legislature to enact them.

Although the issue proved to be less divisive than school consolidation and district reorganization, the Education Reform Act also addressed compulsory school attendance, once one of the most controversial education issues in Mississippi's history.

Legislation enacted in 1918 had made Mississippi the last state in the nation to pass a compulsory attendance law. As weak as this law was, even it had been stricken from the books in 1956, in the midst of Mississippi's civil rights crisis. Tarnished by this action, Mississippi nevertheless continued to get by without such a law until 1977.[54]

Enactment of a new compulsory attendance law in 1977 was primarily a concession to school officials and to education-minded citizens concerned over Mississippi's poor educational achievements. In part, because of continuing fears over close social relations between the races, legislators, as in the past, were reluctant to enact an effective law—the 1977 measure was devoid of funding support or a mechanism for enforcement.

Abundant statistics graphically revealed the consequences of Mississippi's shortsightedness. It was estimated that 6,000 children eligible for entry into first grade during the 1980–81 school year failed to enroll.[55] Compared to the national average of appoximately 13 percent, 20 percent of the state's school-age children were not attending school.[56] Mississippi's dropout rate was roughly 42 percent on the eve of the passage of the Education Reform Act, highest in the nation.[57] Little wonder, then, that Mississippi's adult illiteracy rate in 1978 was the nation's highest or that 35 percent of Mississippi recruits flunked the U.S. Army's standardized test in 1981.[58] Governor Winter, along with other advocates of a stronger compulsory education law, had used data such as these, detailing the wasted human resources and the cause of many of Mississippi's economic and social woes, in his efforts to provoke the passage of a genuine compulsory school attendance law. Lawmakers finally responded.

Beginning with the 1983–84 school year, the Education Reform Act required school attendance for all children who had reached the age of six years, but who had not attained the age of eight years, on or before September 1, 1983. One year of age was to be added each year until the 1989–90 school year, when all children who had reached the age of six, but not yet fourteen, by September 1, were required to attend school. Appropriate penalties were prescribed for violators. Funding was provided for youth or family courts in each county to employ at least one attendance officer who was empowered to carry out the provisions of the act.[59]

The law represented an important milestone for Mississippi education, but it was hardly as strong as reformers wished. Indeed, by national standards it was perhaps the most lenient compulsory attendance law in the country; no other state ended its requirement at the age of fourteen (thirty-three require school attendance until children attain age sixteen, while the remaining states impose attendance until age seventeen).[60] Obvious, too, were the shortcomings inherent in the annual age increments. Many children still did not attend school because they were not immediately affected by the law. In the 1984–85 school year, for example, it is estimated that there were 11,000 dropouts. Had the mandatory age limt of fourteen been in effect in that year, more than 1,900 of that total would have been affected by the law. Approximately 5,500 would have been affected had the law required school attendance to age sixteen.[61]

Other difficulties arose that delayed full implementation of the law. Two years after the enactment, several school districts had no attendance counselors in place. Some court judges, chafing under the legislation because they believed it violated Mississippi's constitutional provisions outlining separation of powers, simply refused to appoint them. Others were concerned that the responsibility of hiring the counselors might subject them to civil liabilities for officers' actions.[62] These problems, however, were soon resolved.

Subsequent legislative action clarified jurisdictional questions and strengthened the law as well. In 1987, lawmakers placed attendance officers under partial control of the State Department of Education, although overall authority remained the responsibility of the county youth-court judges. Of greater consequence, however, was a provision that extended the compulsory attendance law to sixteen-year-olds.[63]

Of course, immediate impact of the law has been negligible. In the 1985–86 school year, for example, the dropout rate of Mississippi schoolchildren fell to 38.2 percent.[64] Figures compiled by the State Department of Education for the 1987–88 school year indicate that 10,533 students dropped out of public schools.[65] With nearly 40 out of every 100 children still not completing secondary school, Mississippi remains near the bottom nationally in that category. But officials are cautiously optimistic that extending the minimum compulsory school age and effectively enforcing the law will eventually lead to the anticipated outcomes—larger numbers of children enrolled in school and remaining there until high school graduation.

Of course, educational leaders understood that keeping students in the classroom was only one step in improving the state's public schools. The quality of their educational experience had to be improved, and it would then have to be effectively measured. Hence, the adequate evaluation of student achievement was central to the reform legislation. The State Department of Education was directed to establish minimum performance standards related to goals in the performance-based school accreditation plan and to implement statewide assessment testing. Each year, students in grades three, five, eight, and eleven were required to be tested in the basic skills areas of reading, mathematics, and writing. The state's curriculum framework, comprising minimum learning objectives that all students had to be taught, served as the basis for the skills tests. State education officials were required to monitor the test results and provide remedial assistance to those districts in which testing deficiencies impacting on district accreditation ratings occurred.[66]

Closely related to the new testing procedures were provisions that mandated each school district to establish new high school graduation requirements. At minimum, the revised standards had to include a requirement for eleventh graders to master minimum performance levels in the basic skills areas, a functional literacy examination to determine student ability to apply those basic skills to everyday life situations, and the completion of a minimum number of academic credits to meet graduation requirements. Students unable to pass the functional literacy examination after proper remediation would not receive a standard high school diploma.[67]

In 1986, third, fifth, and eighth graders, for the first time, completed the Basic Skills Assessment Program test (BSAP). Overall test results were hardly encouraging. More than a third of all fifth and eighth graders—33.2 percent and 36.9 percent, respectively—failed to achieve the minimum passing score of 70 percent in reading skills.[68]

Eleventh graders took the functional literacy examination for the first time in 1985. Test scores revealed that, particularly in mathematics, many students lacked mastery of the minimum skills deemed necessary to function in the larger society. While 8.6 percent failed the reading portion and 9.8 percent failed the written communication portion, more than 45 percent of the high school juniors scored below 70 percent on the mathematics portion of the examination.[69]

Greater efforts in teaching basic skills yielded positive results by 1988; functional literacy examination scores improved considerably. Eleventh graders in the 1987–88 school year passed the reading and written communications sections at the rate of 94.1 percent and 94.8 percent, respectively. Although mathematics scores continued to lag behind the other tested areas, performance here, too, was much improved, with a failure rate of only 10.5 percent.[70] Moreover, compared to the previous year's total of 28.7 percent, 1988 profiles showed that only 7.3 percent of the students failed at least one section of the test.[71]

In the improving educational climate in Mississippi, the state's teachers have finally succeeded in attracting much needed attention to their inadequate pay. In 1982, the average salary for Mississippi teachers was $14,320, nearly $5,000 below the national average.[72] Educators and other public school supporters seldom failed to note such disparities and frequently called attention to the close relationship between good teachers and adequate pay. If the state hoped to improve its schools by attracting and retaining competent educators, it would have to pay them better.

Legislators had addressed teacher pay in the Education Reform Act, but the act endorsed, only in principle, a general goal of raising annual teacher salaries to the southeastern average. Legislators were uwilling to fund more than a $1,000 "across-the-board" increase and minor annual increments for years of teaching experience. The increases were far from what educational advocates sought or teaching professionals expected.[73]

Over the next few years, considerable teacher agitation and solid support from new state leadership resulted in significant teacher pay gains. In 1985, the legislature passed one of the biggest teacher pay raises in the state's history. The legislation increased teacher salaries by $4,400, phased in over a three-year period.[74] The 1985–86 teacher salary averaged $18,443, a 15.8 percent increase over the previous year. But even with the raise, teacher pay remained well below the 1985–86 national average of $25,257, moving ahead only of South Dakota by $348 to occupy the forty-ninth place on the national pay scale.[75] Teachers have fared considerably better in subsequent legislative action, however. In 1988, largely as a result of new Governor Ray Mabus's initiatives and a better state financial climate, the legislature increased teacher pay $3,800 over a two-year span. Consequently, dramatic progress has occurred in this area. Unquestionably, it has boosted teacher morale and given Mississippi a more competitive edge in retaining some of its better classroom personnel. Additionally, the improved salary has influenced good students to enter and former teachers to return to a profession in a state historically impacted by low pay.

With the increase in teacher salaries came a concurrent revision of teacher certification standards. Because a major goal of the Education Reform Act was the improvement of student achievement, more competent teachers and administrators were necessary. Prior to passage of the reform act, teacher certification was based on the completion of a set number of courses in professional and general education areas. As a rule, every five years teachers were required to be recertified by completing a minimum of six semester credit hours of additional prescribed course work. Reform legislation mandated a major modification of both the standards and the methods of teacher and administrator certification and recertification. The act established a commission to develop standards and criteria, subject to approval of the Lay Board of Education, for all teacher education programs, for initial teacher and administrator certification and renewal, and for continuing professional staff development of educational personnel.[76]

To ensure the quality of their offerings, teacher education programs underwent substantial changes. Closely monitored by state education officials, colleges and universities were required to expand their core curriculum for education majors. Before students were formally admitted into a teacher-education program, they were required to meet new minimum standards of grade-point average and to make a satisfactory score on a competency examination that tested their knowledge in basic skills.

The new requirements affected almost immediately the number of students entering into the programs. Especially significant was the impact on blacks, many of whom were unable to make satisfactory scores on the competency examination. But the consequences extended far beyond college campuses. The new standards aggravated an already critical shortage of black educators, ultimately helping to lead to a current "teacher crop which is less reflective of the present racial composition of the State."[77]

Aggravated, too, were already existing teacher shortages. In virtually every field of study, but particularly in science and mathematics, the teacher shortage became acute. The new certification standards proved especially burdensome on the small rural school districts. With few incentives for young educators anyway, they found it next to impossible to attract mathematics and science teachers.[78] As a consequence, the State Department of Education has been forced to issue numerous emergency certificates to existing teaching personnel who do not meet normal certification standards in a particular teaching field. This has hardly been an ideal situation and has raised serious "questions about the overall quality of instruction" some of these teachers are providing.[79]

An entirely new process was developed for teachers and administrators entering the state school system for the first time. For beginning teachers (effective in 1988–89) and beginning administrators (effective in 1989–90), the State Department of Education agreed to issue a one-year provisional certificate. To qualify for provisional teacher status, incoming teachers had to achieve minimum scores (set by state education officials) on the National Teacher Examination on both the core battery and the teacher's cognitive teaching area. The performance of provisional teachers and administrators, closely monitored in their initial year of employment, was to determine their right to a standard certificate and, hence, future employment.[80]

The on-the-job performance of provisional teachers and administrators is evaluated under a process embodied in the Mississippi Teacher/Mississippi Administrator Assessment Instrument. The first statewide uniform evaluation procedures, these teacher and administrator instruments not only have eliminated the various evaluative methods formerly used in districts across the state but also have brought more professional standards into the process.[81] Each provisional teacher is expected to demonstrate mastery of fourteen competencies comprising some forty-two performance indicators. Administrators are evaluated on their mastery of thirteen leadership skills. Failure effectively to demonstrate mastery of all competencies at a prescribed level in the first employment year would result in continuation of provisional status. Such "probationary" individuals were to be frozen at their entry salary level and would have to take advantage of improvement opportunities through a structured remediation process. If the prescribed level of skills had not been mastered after three years of remediation, a provisional employee could no longer receive a certificate and, consequently, would be ineligible to teach or perform administrative duties in the state's public schools.[82]

As with much of the Education Reform Act, it is too early to assess the impact of the new certification procedures on the improvement of the public schools. With the new standards imposed on college educational programs and entering teachers, clearly a moderately adverse effect on teacher supply, especially among minority teachers, has resulted. On the other hand, its potential for significantly improving teacher preparation and instruction is readily apparent. With its emphasis on demonstrated classroom and administrative proficiency, uniformity in evaluating that proficiency, and mandated dismissal as the "ultimate weapon" for those who fail to meet performance expectations, the new process represents an innovative approach in strengthening classroom instruction and school management. It is clearly a departure from Mississippi's educational past.

Essentially the same can be said for the new method of professional staff development. The Education Reform Act mandated a major change in this process. Beginning in the 1984–85 school year, school districts were required to develop and implement state-approved comprehensive plans of staff development. Approval of district plans became the responsibility of the specially created Commission on School Accreditation. The mandatory program of staff activities initiated by the respective school districts were to be "based on institutional needs, and designed to promote continued demonstration of the essential competencies and responsibilities necessary for the district to meet its goals."[83] The new approach was considerably different from the state's previous in-service programs of brief workshops featuring "inspiring speeches and demonstrations of discrete skills." Educational personnel now had to undergo specific staff training and support activities conducted in frequent site workshops and training sessions. Not only would the workshops and sessions focus on teachers and administrators acquiring specific skills and behavior patterns relevant to their school duties, but they were also designed to assist them in assimilating the skills and the information learned.

The ultimate goal of the new process was to facilitate the continuous improvement of school district personnel and to demonstrate that improvement through more effective performance of their responsibilities.[84]

An important component of the performance-based school accreditation system, the new staff development procedures also changed the method of teacher and administrator recertification. Periodic enrollment in college-credit "refresher" courses to satisfy recertification was no longer required. School personnel now had to earn a prescribed number of credits each year through staff development in both training and support activities to meet recertification requirements. Satisfactory completion of these activities automatically would renew certification for one year.[85]

Unquestionably, one area of public education dramatically affected by the reform legislation was school accreditation. Like other specific areas of state public education, it too underwent extensive modification. School accreditation now affected, and was affected by, a large variety of specific educational factors. Perhaps more than any change spurred by the reform law, it represented the clearest philosophical break with past practices and thoughts about the nature, achievement, and measurement of quality public education in Mississippi.

Accreditation standards for schools in Mississippi began in the late nineteenth century. Not until the 1920s, however, did important improvements in the system appear. During that period, a more effective monitoring process was established under the auspices of the Mississippi Education Association and the State Department of Education. In addition, minimum standards for high school programs were created and, for the first time, elementary schools came under the regulatory program. In 1949 the Mississippi Education Association ended its direct role in school accreditation, after the formation of the Mississippi accrediting commission.[86]

These accrediting programs initially applied only to white schools. Accreditation of the separate black public schools was not addressed until 1935. In that year, the Mississippi Association for Teachers in Colored Schools established an accrediting function under its guidance. In 1959, the Negro Accrediting Commission changed its name to the State Accrediting Commission and adopted the same accreditation rules and regulations as the white accrediting agency.[87]

Both groups made extensive use of State Department of Education officials in conducting their voluntary accreditation activities. The lack of direct state responsibility in regulating school programs, however, was hardly an ideal arrangement. Hence, in 1970, following the desegregation of public schools, state law gave the State Department of Education responsibility for school accreditation. But while the law provided for more direct state involvement in the process, it did not mandate accreditation standards for any school in the state; compliance remained strictly voluntary.[88] Moreover, the standards set by the state continued the traditional emphasis on "quantitative factors . . . as the means by which school improvement was to be accomplished."[89] The whole process of accreditation largely involved the measurement of such things as "the lighting in the rooms, the desks, staff members and their qualifications, and the number of books in the library."[90]

Such factors as specific resources and personnel were "assumed" to be sufficient in facilitating high-quality school programs. But mounting educational research soon proved the contrary. The evidence pointed to teacher and administrative performance as significant factors in effective student learning and dictated that accrediting emphasis be "shifted from measures of quantity to those of quality."[91]

This "shift" became the task of a special study group created under the Education Reform Act. Its basic responsibility was to develop a system of accreditation assuring the quality of public schools in compliance with performance-based standards. A permanent performance-based system was required to be fully implemented by the State Board of Education acting through the Commission on School Accreditation not later than July 1, 1986. All public elementary and secondary schools would have to comply with the plan from that day forward.[92]

The law spelled out a minimum number of factors the special task force was to consider in its study of a performance-based school assessment plan.[93] After adopting, field testing, and implementing an approved plan, the State Board of Education was required to establish an accreditation audit unit to visit schools and ascertain compliance with the standards. Audit evaluators, selected, approved, and trained by the Commission on School Accreditation, were required to report the results of their reviews to that agency. Schools failing to meet the prescribed accreditation standards were required by law to undergo a program of development or risk the loss of state funds.

A comprehensive plan of accreditation developed from the Education Reform Act mandate. The system requires all school districts to undergo accreditation visits on a scheduled five-year cycle. Furthermore, they are subject to unannounced random audits to monitor continuous compliance with the standards. All districts must meet prescribed minimum and compulsory performance standards to clear the accreditation process. Performance levels are assigned to districts according to their achievements on the standards. Four different accreditation categories are currently granted by the commission based on the performance level of the evaluated district. Districts assigned to a category indicating deficiencies—the most serious being "accredited-probationary"—must submit, and acquire approval of, a remediation plan. Technical assistance is provided by state educational officials to help eliminate the deficiency(ies), but ultimate responsibility rests with the deficient district. Failure to correct the violation(s) within a specified time results in disaccreditation and, in accordance with state law, a denial of funds until the commission reconsiders the case.[94]

For some state education officials and reform advocates, the performance-based accreditation provision represents "the cornerstone" of the Education Reform Act. But it has not been without its critics, particularly state education officials who find fault with the punitive provision relating to noncomplying districts. Such officials believe that it is necessary to go beyond the mere withholding of funds from disaccredited districts. "To be useful," argues the state superintendent of education, "the laws need to be changed to place the [disaccredited] district under the jurisdiction of the State Board of Education." Such a change "would allow for the removal of the local superintendent and the local board until such time as the district . . . [could] provide a successful school improvement plan which brings the school district back into compliance with state standards."[95]

It is not difficult for Mississippi public education advocates to see the importance of the new performance-based accreditation system in improving the state's schools. With its emphasis on defining and measuring quality education (i.e., of determining how good the teaching is and how well the students are doing), the prospect of positive gains eventually deriving from the system are bright. But while many people in the state regard this provision as the most significant component of the reform legislation, still others see the law's focus on early childhood education as having the greatest potential to improve education in the state.

Mississippians have debated the desirability and feasibility of early childhood education for many years. Prior to enactment of the Education Reform Act, Mississippi stood as the only state in the Union that did not support an early childhood program. Apparently other states were far ahead of Mississippi in their knowledge about the benefits of kindergartens, and from that standpoint alone, one advocate surmised, "early childhood education makes good sense."[96] But it was more than a simple matter of Mississippi needing to play catch-up. For other critics, the lack of a statewide publicly supported kindergarten program lay at the very heart of the state's poorly prepared students and, consequently, Mississippi's poor economic situation. This position had been a part of Governor Winter's campaign message that lay the groundwork for education reform, and supporters did not abandon the theme.

While much of the public was convinced of the need, many of their representatives in the state capital were lukewarm to an extensive kindergarten program. Governor Winter failed to secure passage of a kindergarten bill in two regular legislative sessions, and many of the opponents to the measure remained adamant in their hostility during the educational reform special session.

Although some legislative opponents of kindergartens were convinced that Mississippi simply could not afford such an expensive program, many influential critics had less noble reasons for their opposition. Despite evidence to the contrary, they continued to cling to arguments of the past that kindergartens were nothing more than "unnecessary frills." Frequently, this claim was no more than a mask for an even more obnoxious position.

Aware that blacks constituted the largest proportion of the state's public school enrollment, some legislators balked at the expensive kindergarten provision because they believed whites would derive little benefit. One such legislator opposed the entire reform package largely for that reason, declaring, "Kindergarten would just be day-care centers for blacks."[97]

The kindergarten issue was the most controversial aspect of the legislators' discussion of the reform bill. It consumed the greatest amount of attention and constituted "the heart of the battle" over the entire legislation.[98] Much of the public was aware of that. Perhaps largely for that reason, many Mississippians, unfamiliar with other provisions of the reform law, initially regarded the establishment of kindergartens as the extent of educational reform implemented by the legislation.

Consistent in its focus on improving early childhood education, the reform legislation also provided for a program of reading in the lower elementary grades. The provision called for adding assistant teachers to the classrooms to work under the direction of certified teachers.[99] Similar in some respects to the existing federally funded Chapter I teacher-aide program, the new system differed largely in that it was not limited by the restraints of federal guidelines regarding duties of teacher-aides, and it was to be utilized on a much broader basis in the first three grade levels. Moreover, local districts would have the option of assigning some of the assistant teachers to kindergarten classrooms. The basic idea behind the new assistant-teacher program was to increase the amount of time students could engage in studying and practicing basic skills, especially reading. Assistant teachers were to help facilitate this effort by spending most of their time working with small groups and individual students.[100]

The new program began in the 1983–84 school year. Phased in over a three-year time period, the assistant-teacher program currently employs teachers in all three prescribed grade levels. Although initially some certified teachers were concerned over the prospects of another full-time adult in the classrooms, their qualms soon disappeared. The benefits of the program became readily apparent as teachers and education officials saw performance levels increase in all of the skills areas in those classrooms where teaching assistants were being utilized. In one district, reading scores increased 30 percent after hiring assistant teachers for first-grade classes.[101]

In other areas, too, teachers saw the benefits of the program occur, especially in reinforcing skills and having greater opportunities to work with individual students.[102] Clearly, early indications show that the assistant-teacher program has the potential to have as great an impact on improving education in the lower grades as any provision of the Education Reform Act. It represents one of the most visible signs of educational progress in the state.

Summary and Conclusions

Based upon this review of a historical perspective of educational reform in Mississippi, the following conclusions are indicated:

1. While state executive and legislative leaders have articulated the need for a system of public education, many of the educational statutes have been permissive (laissez-faire), particularly with provisions for local options.
2. State leaders, especially governors, began projecting the relationships between a sound system of public education and economic development during the 1960s. Prior to this time, their support was mostly of a general rhetorical nature.

3. Many of the "reforms" in the Education Reform Act of 1982 represent efforts to make statutory and enabling provisions commonly enjoyed by other states as a part of their minimum education programs.
4. More definitive documentation of the Education Reform Act of 1982 will be possible in the future due to the phased implementation of and legislative changes in the law.

Mississippi's educational code is replete with permissive legislation as documented in the legislative overview sections of this chapter. For instance, the 1846 statute that provided for a uniform and general system of common schools permitted each county to levy taxes in support of such schools. Written consent by a majority of the heads of families in each township was necessary before taxes could be levied. The initial compulsory school attendance law of 1918 provided that the law could be enforced only if 20 percent of the qualified voters in any county petitioned the board of supervisors for a vote on the matter. A majority of the voters, then, had to vote in favor of the petitions in a special election. Even the 1977 comprehensive attendance counseling program, which encouraged school attendance, had no provisions for noncompliance and, therefore, was permissive in effect.

Following publication and transmittal of the Booz-Allen and Hamilton study of Mississippi's system of public education, Governor Paul B. Johnson and subsequent governors articulated the apparent relationship between a sound system of public education and the economic development goals of the state. Prior to this time—with the possible exception of Governor Albert Gallatin Brown, who was strongly supportive of a system of common schools in the 1840s—support for public education was primarily rhetorical by the state executive leadership.

As discussed in the latter section of this chapter, the Education Reform Act included provisions that were commonly enjoyed by other states as a part of their minimum education programs. Mississippi, prior to the Education Reform Act, was the only state in the nation without provisions for statewide early childhood education and a compulsory school attendance law. This lack, it was argued, contributed significantly to the state's inability to report favorable comparative statistics with other state educational programs. Also, Mississippi's inadequate teacher salaries were cited as yet another obstacle to educational improvement that the legislature recognized in the Education Reform Act by stating its intent to raise teacher salaries to the southeastern average.

Although it is too early definitively to assess the impact of the act, there is some indication that the state is beginning to reap some benefits from its implementation. As revealed in an interview with the deputy state superintendent of education, Thomas Saterfiel, (1) Mississippi students are achieving at a higher level, (2) school attendance has improved, especially at the lower grade levels, (3) the scope of the curriculum has changed drastically, (4) American College Test (ACT) scores have been increasing since 1985, and (5) there is a general perception that teachers are better prepared.[103]

Indeed, there appears to be an air of optimism as well as apprehension throughout the state. State Department of Education officials are optimistic that some of the statutes that have limited their effectiveness in facilitating improvement at the local level—such provisions as the election of the county school superintendents, the existence of "no student" school districts, and the operation of very small school districts—will eventually be repealed.

Of course, the road to improvement is not smooth and the Education Reform Act may require modification. There has been citizen opposition to the recommendation by the Educational Finance Commission that the number of school districts be reduced—opposition strong enough to cause this provision to be repealed. Other provisions in the Education Reform Act, such as required compliance with performance-based standards by local school districts, may effectively result in some district reorganization due to the inability of smaller districts to comply.

Nevertheless, it is our position that Mississippi has made a significant departure from its past with the passage of the Education Reform Act and has created a condition for meaningful educational improvement to occur. With the view that significant economic development is inextricably associated with (and dependent upon) a sound system of public education, it should not be difficult for state leaders to gain acceptance of educational improvement proposals in the future.

Educational Reform
in Alabama:
1972–1989

CHARLES F. RUDDER

Reform vs. Improvement

Since the turn of the nineteenth century, education in the United States has been in a process of virtually continuous change. If reform is taken as a synonym for change, the entire history of postcolonial American education could be characterized as a history of educational reform. Charles E. Silberman, in his foreword to *Crisis in the Classroom,* makes the observation that "if every social problem is labeled 'crisis,' we risk losing the ability to distinguish the important from the merely urgent."[1] Similarly, if every educational change is labeled "reform," we risk losing the ability to distinguish replacing or restoring what has become dysfunctional from responding to what is merely in need of immediate attention. If, as we often do, we equate educational change with educational reform, we obscure the significance of the role of history in educational change.[2]

The educational changes proposed by Horace Mann, under his conception of a "common school," incorporated some relatively radical departures from the European educational traditions that had been carried over into most of the colonial schools. If the Common School movement is identified as a period of educational reform, it is important to keep in mind that what was being reformed was as much European as colonial American.

The postrevolutionary criticism and reconstruction of American schools addressed educational traditions that had evolved in the sociohistorical contexts of the Hellenistic, Roman, and European aristocracies and the European clergy. The educational changes, initiated by the Common School movement and continued and elaborated during the Progressive movement, were made in response to the emerging sociohistorical context of life in the New World.[3] This context was shaped by such things as the postcolonial adjustment to becoming a confederation of states, the nation's adjustment to absorbing waves of European and Asian immigrants, westward expansion, and the shift from an agrarian to an industrial economy. These changes, however we currently appraise their pedagogical merit, must be understood as radically different in spirit and intention from, for example, the militarily and technologically motivated proposals for educational change following the launch of Sputnik.

The educational change proposed in the late 1950s and early 1960s were justified by criticism of educational programs that were residues of educational change precipitated by, and made in response to, more than a century of domestic social, political, and educational developments unprecedented anywhere else in the world. These efforts were aimed at changing schools and educational programs that were in many respects uniquely American. It is neither obvious nor insignificant to ask in what sense one is collectively to interpret the Common School movement, the Progressive movement, and post-Progressive educational criticism as instances of actual or attempted educational reform.

Equating the terms reform and change—in addition to eclipsing differences among educational changes relative to the cultural, social, and historical contexts in which they were made—also obscures qualitative distinctions among different types of change. A significant historical and contemporary distinction can be found, for example, between educational changes that are proposed as means of radically altering the *aims* of public education and changes designed to move public schooling toward a more complete realization of pedagogical and curricular goals to which we are already committed.

On the one hand, many changes have been introduced into the schools as attempts to improve education in specific areas where success has been uneven or has not kept pace with progress in other areas. The founding and development of special education and educational counseling, for example, reflect this kind of change. Similarly, the introduction of computer courses and the development of instructional software have been made in an effort, reflecting long-standing commitments, to make instruction more flexible and innovative and to keep the curriculum abreast of scientific and technological development. On the other hand, some calls for educational change are preceded by, or included in, educational criticism alleging that schooling, across the board, has become dysfunctional, malfunctional, or degenerate.

Historically, the principal thrust of educational criticism in the United States has alternated between two contrary charges. Many critics have argued that, as a consequence of cultural inertia, schooling is frozen into traditional forms of organization and practice, rendering it obsolete and unresponsive to current educational demands. Other critics have alleged that, because of public and professional negligence, the quality of schooling has declined from some prior level of excellence. The former charge was influential in the successful struggle to establish compulsory universal public schooling in the United States, while the latter is reflected in the reports on "excellence in education" that surfaced in the early 1980s.

Educational reform, and responses within the educational community to calls for reform, will here be distinguished from other types of educational change and proposals for change. The term "reform" will, hereafter, refer to changes and proposed changes that are designed to reconstruct obsolete and dysfunctional programs or to restore degenerate programs to some prior state of excellence. Educational changes that are proposed as means of maintaining and increasing the continuity of educational development already underway will be identified simply as proposals for educational "improvement." It should be noted that "reform" and "improvement" are typically antithetical. Educational improvement—the continuation, consolidation, and expansion of efforts to achieve goals that have guided the development of current programs—is usually what educational reform opposes and proposes to change.

Post–Civil Rights: 1972–1982

The move toward revising the curriculum and methods of instruction in the public schools following the Sputnik panic was eclipsed after 1962 by the civil rights movement. Consequently, the most significant and durable educational changes in Alabama during the 1960s were made in response to congressional mandates and federal court orders requiring student and faculty desegregation of the public schools. Desegregation and other efforts to eliminate racial discrimination have been and remain critical factors in shaping the course and complexion of public education in Alabama and the nation. Racial discrimination is not, however, rooted in schooling.

The nation's schools were turned to the task of desegregating our social institutions, not because they were blamed for causing segregation, but because schooling is public (universal, compulsory, state-supported, and federally subsidized), which justifies compelling school systems to conform to a strict interpretation of the laws of the land guaranteeing every citizen maximum protection of life, liberty, and pursuit of happiness. Hence, while desegregation (which practically reversed the "separate but equal" rationalization for educational precedents sanctioned by *Plessy v. Ferguson*) fits the profile of reform set out above, it is not taken here as an instance of educational reform per se. The desegregation of public schooling in Alabama, like many educational changes during the Progressive Era, is one among many elements of a more general movement toward social reform.

In the early 1970s, Alabama educators turned their attention to rectifying what they had identified as major discrepancies in teacher certification standards and teacher placement procedures across the state. In 1970, the certification and placement of public school teachers were, at best, haphazard. Holding what William B. Lauderdale has called a laissez-faire attitude toward teacher employment, local superintendents and boards of education could legally issue teaching permits in lieu of certificates and assign certified teachers to positions and grade levels for which they were not certified.[4] In 1972, 20 percent of the teachers in the state were uncertified and 35 percent were teaching out of field.[5] Wide discrepancies also existed in teacher education programs leading to certification among the state's thirty-one institutions offering degrees in education. ACT scores among students in teacher education ranged from 8.5 to 24, and grade-point requirements for admission to teacher education varied from no specific requirement to a minimum requirement of 1.2 on a 3-point scale in all work attempted. At some institutions, the graduation requirements for students in teacher education exceeded university graduation requirements, while at others degrees were issued upon completion of the minimum number of hours required for graduation without regard to the number of hours attempted. The fact that some institutions with as few as four full-time faculty members offered as many as twenty graduate and undergraduate programs leading to teacher certification further exacerbated the problem. For more than a decade, the principal thrust of educational change in Alabama was directed toward establishing statewide uniform standards for preservice teacher education, certification, and placement.

In 1972, the State Board of Education passed a resolution requiring formal board approval of all teacher-education programs in the state and establishing criteria for determining eligibility for program approval. The resolution eliminated teaching "permits" and required that teachers be assigned to positions for which they were certified. Institutions offering degrees in teacher education were required to submit evidence to the board that all of their teacher-education faculty had met the minimum requirements for graduate study in their teaching fields. Minimum ACT/SAT scores and grade-point averages in all work attempted were established for admission to teacher-education programs. The resolution further required that a minimum grade-point average be maintained in all work attempted and established a professional core of studies in educational foundations, minimum requirements for course work in areas of academic specialization, teaching methods, media, and electives as minimum criteria for initial teacher certification.

For three years, colleges and universities in the state adjusted their teacher-education programs to meet the state guidelines for certification even as the guidelines themselves underwent numerous revisions. In 1975, state review teams were organized to determine whether or not state institutions had met the guidelines. Based on these reviews and other evidence of compliance, the state board extended or withheld approval of teacher certification programs in the state's colleges and universities.

The last and most controversial move to upgrade teacher certification in Alabama came in the form of a resolution passed by the State Board of Education in 1978 requiring the development of a minimum competency test to be used as the last step in screening applicants for initial teacher certification. Three years in development, the Alabama Initial Teacher Certification Test (AITCT) was officially administered for the first time in 1981. The performance of graduates of schools across the state varied considerably, and, in December 1981, a lawsuit alleging racial bias in the test was filed against the state. In the spring of 1987, the U.S. Eleventh Circuit Court of Appeals upheld the use of the AITCT but set guidelines for interpreting test scores under which the instrument failed to discriminate significantly among any of those who had taken the test as part of their application for initial teacher certification. As a consequence, the state dropped the test.

The summary of educational changes in Alabama set out above is intended to indicate only what was most characteristic of educational change in the state between 1972 and 1982. The pedagogical, curricular, and administrative details of the new guidelines for teacher certification in Alabama are legion and under constant revision. The essential point here is that educational leaders in the state did not present these changes as designed to reverse a massive decline in the quality of education in Alabama or to remedy uniformly low standards of teacher preparation and certification. The problem the new guidelines were designed to solve was that of uneven performance among teacher-education programs in the state. The move to establish uniform standards for certification in Alabama was not made in response to a national or local public mandate for change, and the changes required by the new guidelines were not made in teacher-training institutions or local school systems under any sense of urgency or the need to justify (or rejustify) public education.

Truman M. Pierce, dean emeritus of the Auburn University College of Education and author of the first draft of what was to become the 1972 State Board of Education resolution, did refer to the resolution as a state reform of teacher education. However, his description and justification of the process set in motion by the resolution fit the profile of a proposal for educational *improvement.* According to Dean Pierce, the resolution was designed to help Alabama achieve further progress toward realizing previously established and currently accepted goals. Pierce, a graduate of Teachers College at Columbia University in the late 1940s, was seriously dedicated to the ideals of progressive education as he understood them. In 1978, he went to some length to describe the changes recommended in the new guidelines as a continuation of the historical progress in American public education, beginning with the "common school" and continuing through the Progressive movement, toward the democratization of public schooling and the professionalization of teaching.[6]

In the spring of 1978, four articles—by Pierce, the state superintendent of education, a member of the State Board of Education, and a representative of the Alabama State Department of Education—were published in the *Professional Educator* and were optimistic about what had been accomplished in Alabama since the 1972 resolution and about the future of public education in the state.[7] These spokesmen shared the view that, while much remained to be accomplished, real and pressing problems had been addressed and progress toward their solution was well under way. Especially significant was the implicit assumption behind this optimism that existing educational resources, including current teachers and undergraduate and graduate programs in teacher education, were at least adequate for making significant progress in the future. In short, the rhetoric of educational change in Alabama during the 1970s was not the rhetoric of reform.

The Turn to Reform: 1983–1989

Not since the post-Sputnik indictments of American public education in the late 1950s and early 1960s have critics of education launched such scathing and wholesale attacks on the nation's schools as those found in the rash of reports on "excellence in education" published in the early 1980s. The frequently cited introductory remarks in the report by the National Commission on Excellence in Education, *A Nation at Risk,* bear repeating in order to underscore the scope, the depth, and the gravity of the educational decadence that, the commission alleged, gripped our public schools:

> We report to the American people that . . . the educational foundations of our society are presently being eroded by a rising tide of mediocrity that threatens our very future as a nation and a people. . . . If an unfriendly power had attempted to impose on America the mediocre educational performance that exists today, we might well have viewed it as an act of war. . . . We have, in effect, been committing an act of unthinking, unilateral educational disarmament.[8]

In the wake of this report, described by Henry A. Giroux as "one of the most important reform documents of the last decade," school systems around the nation responded by setting out in pursuit of excellence.[9]

Alabama's quest for excellence was initiated in 1984 by a State Department of Education mandate entitled "A Plan for Excellence," followed in the same year by a legislatively mandated "Career Incentive Program." Two years later, The University of Alabama and Auburn University accepted invitations to join the Holmes Group Consortium of Research Universities.

Alabama's 113-page "Plan for Excellence" had been set in motion by the creation of thirty-four task forces run by nearly one thousand volunteers and charged with finding the ways and means of implementing reforms. What they found, as it is represented in the "Plan for Excellence," was the need for a longer school day, required homework in each subject area, statewide kindergarten, and the elimination of social promotions. Revised high school graduation requirements reduced the number of types of high school diplomas from three to two—standard and advanced. Both diplomas included more units in science and fewer in physical education. The advanced diploma included an additional unit in mathematics, science, and social studies, with a corresponding 2½-unit reduction in electives.[10]

All of the changes set out above conform to the recommendations set out in *A Nation at Risk* under the headings "Content," "Expectations," and "Time," and the graduation requirements equal or exceed the report's guidelines.[11] The state also followed the report's advice on enlisting community support. For example, local communities and civic groups were encouraged by the state superintendent to accommodate the move toward excellence by discontinuing such things as Little League games on school nights. Parents were advised to brace themselves for supervising more homework and were cautioned to expect an increase in retention rates, which one city superintendent estimated could run as high as 30 percent.

The Alabama legislature responded to the national search for excellence with the Education Reform Act of 1984. This act created the Governor's Education Reform Commission, which was, among other things, charged with the development of an incentive-pay plan for teachers and a statewide teacher evaluation system. A commission subcommittee, chaired by the state superintendent of education, combined these charges by recommending legislation that would establish the Alabama Career Incentive Program—a career-ladder plan for regulating retention, tenure, and promotion, based on statewide teacher evaluations. In the following year, the teacher evaluation system was developed and a crash program of evaluator training was completed. The evaluation instrument was administered during the 1986–87 school year after which it was to be normed on the data collected during that year.

Like the "Plan for Excellence," the Education Reform Act also conformed closely to the reform agenda set out in *A Nation at Risk*. Under "Recommendations for Teaching," that document had specifically recommended tying salary, promotion, tenure, and retention decisions to an evaluation system.[12] It had also proposed the development of career ladders that ranked teachers as "beginning," "experienced," and "master."

Much of this movement came to an abrupt halt in the face of unexpected (and apparently unrelated) political developments in the state. During the gubernatorial race in 1986, internecine conflict so divided the Alabama Democratic party that for the first time in almost a century the Republican candidate, Guy Hunt, was elected governor of Alabama. The new governor immediately let it be known that he was not prepared automatically to reendorse the educational policies of the preceding administration. During the first year of his term in office, Governor Hunt initiated a reevaluation of state educational priorities and problems focused primarily on the issue of the administrative organization of the state universities and junior colleges. From the beginning, Governor Hunt seemed, at most, lukewarm about the Career Incentive Program.

Early in the 1988 legislative session, Governor Hunt recommended to the legislature that the Education Reform Act be repealed. A motion to repeal the act passed in both houses by a substantial margin. In the fall of 1989, the State Department of Education announced that it was revising the teacher evaluation system: that it would be submitted to local school systems as a set of guidelines and that teacher evaluation would not be used as a uniform standard for retention, tenure, and promotion decisions. In four years much of Alabama's enthusiasm for reform had waxed and waned. Approaching the turn of the decade, Alabama appeared to be returning to a course of action that was, like the 1970s, more influenced by local concerns, problems, and controversies related to the history of educational development in Alabama than by a national agenda of educational reform.

It remains to be seen what the effect of the Holmes Group on teacher education and the professional roles of public school teachers might be. It is noteworthy, however, that the repeal of the Education Reform Act and the revised function of teacher evaluation indicate a diminished base of support for the career ladder—a notion central to the Holmes Group agenda. This diminished support, in turn, would appear to weaken the base of support for the Holmes Group's change strategy, which the group had taken to be one of its major strengths.

The Holmes report argues that, in the past, proposals for change failed because they worked for piecemeal changes in specific areas or isolated programs rather than for coordinated changes across a range of areas and programs. Hence, the Holmes Group has insisted, the success of its agenda for change requires coordinated simultaneous or sequential changes in colleges of education, colleges of arts and sciences, state departments of education, and local school systems.[13] It currently appears that, in Alabama, at least two of these—the State Department of Education and local school systems—are moving away from the Holmes ideal and are therefore unlikely candidates for cooperation in programs designed to achieve the goals of the Holmes Group.

Another significant factor in the future success of the Holmes Group Consortium in Alabama is the sensitivity of educational programs to state political pressures, which, as we have seen, were instrumental in killing the Career Incentive Program and stalling the AITCT. That the Alabama State Department of Education, local school systems, public school teachers, and the general public will put the priorities of a national association of deans of colleges of education above the practical demands of the state's economy, demographics, social problems (such as juvenile single parents and juvenile crime), and party politics seems highly improbable. Unless the Holmes Group Consortium is able to raise its initial point of contact in Alabama to a more politically powerful level than that of university administration, its influence is most likely to be contained within the traditionally restricted domains of influence of the two affiliated state universities.

After 1983, proposals for educational change in Alabama shifted from the continuing effort to improve public education in the state to those designed to reverse an educational history of mediocrity and indifference to excellence in education. In 1978, the state superintendent of education had written, "When I was appointed State Superintendent, one of my priorities was to support the continuation of progress in teacher education which had been led by [my predecessor] Dr. Leroy Brown."[14] He had gone on to characterize this progress in terms of "actions which were designed to improve the opportunities for boys and girls to learn and grow."[15] Yet, in 1984, without ever acknowledging that public education in Alabama had deteriorated in the 1960s and 1970s, this same state superintendent was leading the charge to implement the "Plan for Excellence," which, in every major respect, conformed to recommendations set out by educational critics who sought to reverse the effects of twenty years of negligence and educational irresponsibility.

In launching his plan for excellence, the state superintendent incorporated the critics' recommendations while marshaling public support created by the news media. This approach left reflective teachers and members of the general public to conclude that the "Plan for Excellence" was issued either for political expediency or as a response to an educational crisis in Alabama.

The Education Reform Act put teachers and the public in the same position. Virtually overnight, the people of Alabama were expected to change their thinking about public education relative to proposals for improving the public schools. Within a period of less than five years the rationale for educational change had changed. The new justification for educational change turned on a reinterpretation of the history of education in Alabama since the late 1950s. What had been characterized as a period of uneven educational progress was now represented as a period of negligence resulting in an educational mediocrity and constituting a serious threat to our national economic and political security. By the mid-1980s, the rhetoric of change had become the rhetoric of reform.

Calls for Reform: The Aftermath

The press for educational reform in the 1980s was justified by a three-pronged attack on public education that focused on (1) the public school curriculum, student evaluation, and graduation requirements, (2) teacher education programs, and (3) teacher placement, promotion, and tenure policies. As we have seen, in Alabama only the first of these revisions has been even approximated, and the prospect of significant statewide changes on the other two fronts appears remote. The consequences of Alabama's reform efforts must, therefore, be examined in light of the current failure to achieve what had been attempted. At least three broad consequences of Alabama's responses to the recent calls for educational reform might shed some light on why plans laid for Alabama's quest for excellence in education have, for the most part, aborted.

One consequence of the reform effort has been to put the educational leadership of the state in the position of having to redesign educational programs without the benefit of prior experience as a guide. In the 1970s, the state's educational leaders could, like Dean Pierce, evaluate programs in terms of practical criteria of effectiveness that had been repeatedly submitted to the scrutiny of critical scholarship and research and that had had some history of success. What's more, teachers could relate to these criteria. Under the reform agenda, educational administrators were forced to rely exclusively on the assumptions and ideological tenets of the reform documents themselves as the criteria for judging the educational merit of established programs as well as proposals for change.

A second consequence of the shift to educational reform in Alabama, like the abortive attempts radically to revise the curriculum and teaching methods following the launching of Sputnik, has been its short life expectancy as a source of educational planning. The Career Incentive Program, for example, is now dead in the water. This shortsightedness has resulted in an almost zero return on an enormous investment of educational resources—financial and human—that went into the development of that program.

A third consequence of Alabama's response to calls for educational reform has been to expose the vulnerability of public school programs to arbitrary shifts in the climate of political opinion and the ideological influence of national and state political platforms. This is apparent in the rise and fall of Alabama's Education Reform Act during the administrative shift from the Democratic to the Republican party and in the fate of the AITCT.

Recent years have seen virtually no substantial difference between the Democratic and Republican platforms in Alabama. While Alabama traditionally has been Democratic (and Guy Hunt is the first Republican governor in over 100 years), a shift in party affiliation implies no ideological shift there. For example, Fob James, a longtime Republican, became a Democrat for the sole purpose of capturing the popular vote for governor in 1978. This same course was followed by Charles Graddick, who was elected attorney general in 1982 on the Democratic ticket (he later returned to the Republican party after being disqualified by the Democratic party in his 1986 bid for governor, due to voting irregularities). Whenever incumbents are defeated, regardless of party affiliation, many of their programs are scrapped as a means of weakening the opposition's practical influence under the new administration and campaign platform in future elections. While such shifts may be strategically expedient in the political arena, they often disrupt the continuity of public programs in ways that are, relative to the aims of these programs, arbitrary and counterproductive.

The deviation in Governor Hunt's educational policy from the national agenda for educational reform, set by a Republican administration and supported by Hunt's Democratic predecessor, was not publicly explained or defended on pedagogical grounds or in terms of any public critique of the reform movement. Hence, the deviation from the national reform agenda in educational policy in Alabama after 1985 supports the contention that public educational policy under the Hunt administration was driven by a pedagogically arbitrary political expediency that put a higher priority on local power struggles than national party loyalty.

The educational influence of power politics in Alabama continues to be dictated by the inertia of tradition, periodically and temporarily disrupted by calls for educational and social reform. The press for reform, when it has been influential, has typically been so as a consequence of a real or contrived social crisis. The temporary revision of curricular and pedagogical goals in the late 1950s and early 1960s, for example, was buttressed by the rhetoric of cold war politics that fostered and exploited public fears of Soviet and Chinese military aggression. These efforts were eclipsed during the civil rights movement when educational programs had to be adjusted to meet the more concrete and immediately pressing demands of disenfranchised citizens. As educational programs began to restabilize in the 1970s, the focus of educational policies returned to practical local issues and to matters that had been subjects of professional educational concern since midcentury. The discontinuity and shortsightedness revealed in Alabama's recent public education reform moves are, I believe, rooted in external political manipulation of public school programs that is indifferent to the internal pedagogical goals of those programs— goals pertaining to the historical efforts within the educational community to professionalize public education.

The Conflicting Aims of Professional Education and Academic Reform

Whatever political advantages may have attended Alabama's educational reform efforts, they were contrary to the aims of professionalism in public education. The primary goal of the movement to professionalize public school teaching has not been higher wages or improved working conditions; it has been to improve the effectiveness of classroom teachers by means of scholarship and research directed toward an increased understanding of the relationship between teaching and learning, communicated to teachers and other practitioners through a professional literature and studies in teacher education.

Elevating the occupational status and performance of public

school practitioners from "wage earner" to "professional" has long been accepted by administrators and teachers as a major means of improving the overall quality of public education. This agenda has been evident in the move of teacher education from normal schools to teachers colleges and universities, in the initiation and development of educational studies and research, in the introduction of graduate studies in education, in the evolution of certification standards and state licensing procedures, and in the educational evaluation movement.

The move toward educational reform in the 1980s in Alabama reflects a betrayal of the theoretical and practical goals of professional education on at least two counts. First, it supported educational changes justified by many assumptions about effective teaching and teacher education that are no longer tenable in light of modern experience and scholarship. That is to say that many of the proposed changes were in conflict with the conclusions of pedagogical inquiry and research that constitute the knowledge base for the professional training of public school teachers and administrators. Second, the shift to educational reform in Alabama was made without any publicly acknowledged scholarly review and evaluation of either the proposals for reform or of the proposed changes in public school practice that were mandated in the alleged effort to improve public education. That is, no attempt was made to appraise critically the conflicting aims of professional education and the agenda for educational reform. A parallel can be found in Alabama's response to the desegregation order of an earlier time.

The move to desegregate the public schools in Alabama during the 1960s reflected both the spirit and the intention of Horace Mann's vision of a "common school" and John Dewey's conception of "progressive education" as well as the contemporary understanding of the aims of a democratic society. Moreover, professional education studies, in such fields as philosophy and history of education, educational psychology, sociology, anthropology, educational counseling, and curriculum and instruction, were saturated with terminology, principles, and recommendations for practices that reflect democratic aims. Despite the constructive consequences of the efforts to desegregate Alabama's schools, the fact that it was done only in reaction to legal coercion (rather than as a reflective effort guided by educational inquiry to achieve commonly accepted educational goals) is evidence of the failure of Alabama educational administrators to respond professionally to external political pressures. The administrators of public education in Alabama and, under their leadership, Alabama teachers failed to practice what they had preached and what they had learned, or had occasion to learn, from personal and collective experience and professional studies in the history and practice of pedagogy. The same failure, namely the failure to respond professionally to national and state political developments and pressures, is apparent in the response of Alabama educators to the calls for educational reform during the 1980s.

The response of Alabama educators to calls for educational reform after 1980 failed the test of professionalism on virtually all counts. The most obvious failure is apparent in the unaddressed contradictions between public assessments of educational progress and the future of public education in Alabama that were made by the state superintendent and others during the 1970s and the rationale for change mandated by the same superintendent during the 1980s. The tacit, unaddressed contradictions into which the educational leaders in Alabama were forced by their response to the call for reform, however politically expedient that response may have been, made this response fundamentally irrational and unprofessional.

The leaders might have asked many questions. They might have asked for a critical review and appraisal of the reports on excellence in education from educational historians, philosophers, evaluators, and researchers in an effort to distinguish claims that were warranted from those that were not, as well as those that were relevant to Alabama from those that were not. They might have asked if the problems that were identified were primarily educational problems or if they were the result of multiple historical, social, political, economic, and educational factors beyond the control and influence of public educators. They might have asked why the educational changes that had only recently been made in the state could not, in time, be expected to yield some, if not all, of the results called for by the reformers. They might have asked why the reformers were confident that their proposals were more likely to succeed than previous attempts at reform that, for the most part, have had a dismal history of success. They might have asked why we could not expect a more reasonable prospect of educational success under persistent efforts to identify and explore a *variety* of approaches to solving educational problems. They might have asked how the changes proposed by the reformers would affect the dropout rate in Alabama, which was (and remains) one of the highest in the nation.

To have responded in the manner suggested above would have represented a rational response to criticism. And it would have countered the attack on the credibility of education as a profession by questioning the credibility of the critics. This response would have been possible if educators had been committed to a theory of rational criticism grounded in the rationality of questioning within the context of critical conversation.[16]

As it stands, there is really nothing new to be learned from the Alabama experience in dealing with educational change during the last fifteen years. There has been no deviation from the basic pattern of education that has marked education for the nation at large since the Common School movement. *This is not to say, however, that there is nothing instructive about it.* What I have tried to show is that we are currently as much in need of a general theory of education as we were in Dewey's day, and for the same reasons.

As Dewey saw it, education would remain in what he described its "empirical" form for as long as it remained devoid of a coherent general theory by means of which it could be lifted to scientific (which, for Dewey, just meant intelligently or rationally guided) status:

> Nobody would deny that education is still in a condition of transition from an empirical to a scientific status. In its empirical form the chief factors determining education are tradition, imitative reproduction, response to various external pressures

wherein the strongest force wins out, and the gifts, native and acquired, of individual teachers. In this situation there is a strong tendency to identify teaching ability with the use of procedures that yield immediately successful results, success being measured by such things as order in the classroom, correct recitation by pupils in assigned lessons, passing of examinations, promotion of pupils to a higher grade, etc.[17]

Dewey's description of the attitudes and beliefs that dominated educational decision making in 1929 is as accurate today as it was sixty years ago. We continue to look to public education for a "quick fix" to immediate problems. In the long run, this mistake has left us with a history of short-term "episodes" of educational adjustment.

Concluding Postscript

Conspicuously absent in our thinking about public education has been an adequate conception of educational continuity. Our preoccupation with empirical immediacy has produced an exaggerated "present" orientation. We tend to view everything we do in terms of its immediate utility; what makes sense in general is what makes sense now. This approach to change and development lends itself well to a cumulative linear (mechanical) concept of social progress—a notion implicit in the idea of excellence and educational reform promoted in Alabama and fundamental to most, if not all, of the educational models that derive from educational psychology and measurement.

In contrast with the mechanical/linear view of progress is the view of human rationality and rational personal and social development suggested by the inherent rationality of questioning/conversation. Genuine conversation, which may be more a matter of listening than of speaking, is not a sequence of monologues. It is characterized by slow and uneven development, the necessity of mutual respect for all participants, a tolerance for the shock of unpopular or foreign ideas, reversals and rereversals of opinion as conversation progresses, the need to review past discussions in order periodically to reestablish the conversational ground and to incorporate new participants into the conversation, the moral resilience to overcome offense, wounded pride, and arrogance, and the absence of a predetermined end or final outcome.

As a theoretical guide or leading conception of the educative process, *conversation* seems to have an advantage over empirical conceptions of teaching, learning, and public decision making. It reflects an organismic conception of education as a social process. Unlike the linear metaphor of progress, which views the public schools as moving with (or even propelling society toward) some higher goal, the organismic vision of the mission of public education is one of adaptation to the pressures, demands, and opportunities presented by the broader social environment.

For those who take an organismic approach to social evaluation and planning, human groups as well as individual human beings are viewed as being alive as opposed merely to being organized. This approach, in turn, means that we must identify life and living in ways that go beyond the biological and material conditions that support life. These conditions are identifiable as the aesthetic and moral factors that figure so prominently in the circumstances of human life—the conditions that determine the quality of individual and community living.

Affluence and organization (designed to promote and protect affluence) are not, in themselves, sufficient for securing and protecting the quality of human existence. Beyond military and industrial bookkeeping and even academic accountability lie the more fundamental questions concerning personal freedom, integrity, and social justice. These too are the responsibility of education. An educational course charted on the assumption that aesthetic and moral concerns are self-tending is just as treacherous as one that grows negligent in its attention to technical interests.

The fundamental educational problem that emerges out of the tension between aesthetic and moral interests, on the one hand, and technical interests, on the other, is the problem of ordering priorities. However, it is not a question of either-or, nor is it a question of *balancing* priorities. For public education, it is a political question—a question of coming to public agreement on priorities, and, in a society dedicated to the growth of democracy, it is imperative that it be an uncoerced, voluntary agreement. Two conditions, at the very least, must be met if a government predicated on popular sovereignty is to survive: patriotism (the loyalty of the people to the state) must be uncoerced, and impediments to popular access to, and influence in, public debate must be eliminated. If we fail to meet these conditions, democracy fails.

If we hold that a primary responsibility of public education in the United States is to promote a more democratic society, we must see that the success of public schooling is contingent on the progressive elimination of circumstances that erode the public trust and the free exchange of ideas. A primary means by which the public is made aware of conditions in our society that are detrimental to the growth of public trust in our social, political, and economic institutions is public dispute. From the organismic point of view, public controversy must be taken as a sign of public health. Hence, calls for the reform of public education and critical questioning of these calls must be taken as signs of life and social vitality. Neither the would-be reformers nor their critics are destructive to education.

That the history of American education is a history of disputation and partial (even piecemeal and temporary) resolution of conflict is a positive vital sign. And it is no small achievement that, despite our educational struggles, we have managed to maintain a system of public schooling that is, as Lauderdale points out, the educational foundation for a people who

> enjoy a standard of living that is the envy of the entire world. [Who] are protected by one of the most powerful and sophisticated military establishments in history. [Who] are informed by a news media that is second to none in freedom, diversity and aggressiveness. [Who] are first in the world in gross national product, imports, and exports. . . . [A people who lead] the world in agricultural productivity. . . . [Who] lead the world in total Olympic medals won. [Who] lead the world in Nobel prize winners, except for literature. . . . [Who] have more foreign students

attending our universities than anyone in the world. [Whose] symphony orchestras consistently receive international acclaim; . . . [and who] have created art forms, such as jazz, that are enjoyed and imitated the world over. And the list goes on.[18]

"These are not," Lauderdale continues, "the accomplishments of a nation of idlers."[19] They are also not the marks of a national program of education that has failed to make and maintain progress.

This progress is reflected in the schools of Alabama. Even measures of student achievement that have, in recent years, equaled or exceeded national norms are testimony to the fact that Alabama students share the educational affluence of our nation. This same progress, however, is just as likely to alienate those among us who remain shackled by poverty and victimized by bigotry and institutionalized patterns of discrimination as it is to encourage those of us who are its benefactors. If in the process of attempting to right social wrongs we find that we must, for a time, sacrifice material efficiency for the sake of improving the quality of community life, as perhaps we did during the civil rights movement, we must be prepared to accept this as a period of recuperation in much the same way that we accept it in the case of physical illness. The democratic premise is that, given the opportunity, human beings will respond. And the recovery of equilibrium among the school systems in Alabama following the dislocation and stresses of desegregation, for black and white families alike, is evidence that in Alabama this faith has not been misplaced. Much remains to be accomplished, and in solving old problems new problems are created. Reform movements call attention to problems, but they cannot dictate solutions. The challenge of reform in Alabama has been, and will remain, a test of our commitment to face our problems and to assess our strengths in order that we may channel our best resources into paths that will move us closer to solving these problems.

The Illusion
of Educational Reform
in Georgia

WAYNE J. URBAN

This chapter is a commentary on the recent school "reform" legislation that was unanimously passed by the Georgia legislature in early 1985. The school bill was based on a recommendation from the governor that was, in turn, based on the report of his own Governor's Education Review Commission. That commission, in its first of two printed reports to the governor, stated that its recommendations represented "a consensus view of over 1,000 educators, business people, and parents."[1] This large, though selective, base (one wonders about labor, minorities, and other possibly unrepresented groups, perhaps even students) has been reinforced in its influence by the nonstop rhetoric from the Atlanta newspapers supporting passage of the bill. Their seeming decision simply to adopt the point of view of the governor and his commission and to make sure that the legislature did not trifle with the recommendations for reform indicates the existence of a powerful coalition of established individuals and groups seeking to force their will on our schools, their teachers, and students.

The push for reform in Georgia is not unique to this state. Governors and legislatures in several states, particularly southern states, have engaged in similar efforts to upgrade their school systems. The tendency of these reforms to be punitive to the teaching force is more likely to occur in the South, with its relatively weak teacher organizations, than in other regions of the country, with more established and influential teacher organizations. Yet, the story of school reform is more than an account of teacher organizations. Educational reform has been in the air everywhere in the United States, much of it in response to a national push for "educational excellence." Let us see what this push means in one state where the governor is staking his reputation on the changes that will be made in the schools.

Two major points will be argued in this chapter. The first is that the "reform" aspects of the Georgia education bill are overrated in significance—not only in relation to the reform commission recommendations but also taken as a whole. The second is that the bill represents a quite controversial approach to American education, particularly when considered from a historical perspective. Several aspects of the reform represent the industrialization of the American school, a movement pernicious in its effects on students, teachers, and parents.

The first point, pertaining to the relative insignificance of the reforms, is illustrated, particularly, in the comparison of the bill with the rhetoric of its advocates. Despite the contention of the governor, members of the reform commission, and the Atlanta newspapers that the bill must go through the legislature unscathed in order to maintain the purity of the reform effort, it was materially weakened at the hands of the governor himself. A prime example of this weakening related to the issue of election or appointment of school superintendents. In its report, the governor's commission made a cogent case for changing the method of choosing superintendents in school districts from election to appointment. Saying a great deal in a few words, the commission noted that "appointment would ensure candidates whose qualifications were primarily professional rather than the ability to marshall funds for a political campaign and would also make Superintendents less susceptible to political pressure."[2] Not only would this change make superintendents less susceptible to political pressure but, in turn, it would also lessen unwarranted political intrusions into the affairs of principals and teachers. In fact, this one change would have brought Georgia into the twentieth century in its local administrative arrangements. But, alas, it was not to be.

Before going to the legislature, the governor evidently read the political signs emanating from the rural county courthouses and deleted this recommendation from the bill.

A second example of failed reform occurs in the bill's recommendations in the area of vocational education. Both the commission report and the legislative enactment of its recommendations reflect dissatisfaction with vocational education. Yet, this dissatisfaction is hardly resolved by the provisions of the bill. The law calls for the discontinuation of job training in vocational classes in all grades except the twelfth. Instead of job training, it recommends career awareness experiences and "increased emphasis on vocationally relevant basic academic skills (reading, writing, math, science)" at all secondary levels. The commission, the governor, and the legislature came close here to dealing with one of the great shell games of American education—the vocational education shell game—but shrank from the consequences of their discovery. They identify several long-standing problems in vocational education when they state that "in-depth training for specific jobs may be outmoded by the time the student gets on the job," "the State does not have the resources for state-of-the-art equipment and expertise required for advanced training at the secondary level," and "time spent on such training may be counter-productive if pursued at the expense of greater mastery of the basic skills."[3] One might expect that these criticisms would lead to the recommendation that vocational education be eliminated from the public schools or, at least, curtailed severely. The validity of the career awareness experiences called for by the commission is undemonstrated, and the notion of reading, writing, math, and science as vocationally relevant implies, needlessly, that the skills should be taught in separate vocational courses or sections. Of course, skill and knowledge in these areas is relevant, but this does not mean that these subjects should be taught separately to vocational students. Could it be that the strength of the vocational education lobby, which is based on the strength of business and industry in the state, caused the educational reformers to abandon the consequences of one of their most significant recommendations?

Finally, the recommendation for equalization in school funding is another area where the timidity of this reform package is made clear. In Georgia, we have tried, at least twice in the last quarter century or so, to equalize educational funding provisions by district. Each time we have failed. Neither the Minimum Foundations Program of the late 1940s nor the Adequate Program for Education in Georgia, during Governor Jimmy Carter's administration, were funded sufficiently to achieve their objective. What real evidence do we have that the latest effort to equalize school funding will succeed where the others have failed? Certainly, it does not come from the legislature. There is also evidence that funds provided to districts by the legislature under provisions of the Quality Basic Education program are being misused.[4]

The second major point of this chapter is that several of the provisions in the reform package are harmful and represent the industrialization of the school room. This metaphor of industrialization highlights the fact that the provisions of the bill are geared to prescribing in more and more detail what is to be expected of students and teachers in the schools at all levels in all subjects. The outcome of this process is likely to be schooling that is rote, mechanical, lifeless, and illiberal, but it will be measured, tested, and evaluated quite precisely. Students will be robbed of any diversity in their classroom experiences that might have led them to link their learning to some variety, value, and stimulation in their lives.

A major illustration of this point occurs in the call for a mandated statewide curriculum. The reform bill stipulates that: "The State Board of Education shall adopt a uniformly sequenced core curriculum for grades kindergarten through 12. All local units of administration shall include this uniformly sequenced core curriculum as the basis for their own curriculum."[5] On the same page, the bill goes on to provide for periodic review of the core curriculum and the student "competencies" on which the review is to be based. While the matter of competencies will be dealt with later in this chapter, suffice it to say that the severe centralization of curriculum making called for in the bill deprives the local schools of this responsibility and gives it to the State Department of Education. The effect of this shift is to weaken the voice of students, teachers, and parents. We have here a continuation of what Arthur E. Wise calls the bureaucratization of the American classroom.[6] This process will encourage roteness and rigidity in the study of subjects in Georgia schools unless it is substantially ignored by the teachers and the students.

Another aspect of reform that will affect students' class experiences negatively is the provision for frequent standardized tests. The reform bill mandates "nationally norm-referenced" tests in "grades two, four, seven, and nine" and state-developed "criterion-referenced instruments" in grades "one, three, six, eight, and ten." One wonders what happened to the fifth grade and, further, whether teachers and students will flock to the fifth grade and wish to stay there, safely protected from the testers. The bill also requires that a test be developed for students entering the first grade in order to indicate whether or not students are truly ready for that experience. (So much for the developmental aspects of kindergarten instruction.) Given this overemphasis on testing, one wonders whether anything besides testing will go on in the classrooms. What will become of teaching and learning for their own sakes? Or for any other reason besides performance on some kind of standardized test? Is it not likely that we will see teachers learn how to teach children to pass tests, without necessarily, or perhaps even probably, learning the things that passing the test implies that they know?[7] We have a precedent for this testing emphasis in England in the nineteenth century. It was known as the system of "payment by results," where teachers were paid on the basis of student answers to test questions put to them by examiners. the outcome of that system was teaching to the test and deemphasis on any other kind of learning in the schools.[8] It proved to be a most unsatisfactory system and had to be abandoned. The main beneficiary of the testing emphasis in the Georgia reform bill seems to be the testing industry. It is doubtful that either students or the state at large will benefit.

Of course, it is not just students who will be tested as a result of this reform. Teachers are to be tested in a variety of ways:

subject matter exams, general knowledge exams, and performance or competency-based instruments. This last variety of examination is deserving of special consideration because, unlike the other two types of tests, it represents a major step toward the de-skilling of teachers. The existing Georgia Teacher Performance Assessment Instrument (TPAI) was developed a few years ago to isolate the individual behaviors that teachers should exhibit and then to evaluate them on whether or not they do exhibit such behaviors in their teaching. This is exactly the opposite of what should be happening in classrooms. Instead of emphasizing the variety of problems and issues that will be encountered in classrooms and the developing of general understandings and strategies that a teacher might use to deal with this variety, performance-based instruments pay attention to mechanical behaviors prescribed by the test developers. One wonders what college instructors would do if they were evaluated on such TPAI categories as "questioning" or "enthusiasm." The triviality of the approach has a certain virtue, that is, its objective character—either teachers exhibit the behavior or they don't—but it also contains the vice of being simple, mechanistic, and ultimately unrelated to the important aspects of teaching and learning going on in classrooms.

The rationale for this kind of evaluation is that it makes teachers and schools accountable for what is learned. The real accountability, however, is that of a bookkeeping system. If we break everything down into its particular parts and make sure that the parts are covered, we will solve the problem of teaching and learning. But are not these areas where the whole is equal to more than the sum of its parts? The parts that are isolated by the performance-based evaluation systems are not even the significant parts of teaching. The consequence of this kind of evaluation is to take control of the classroom away from the individual teacher by prescribing the teacher's behaviors. Couple this with the assumption of control over the curriculum by the State Department of Education, and the de-skilling of the teacher will be complete.[9] It is ironic that at the same time that we talk of raising standards for getting into teaching (and the bill does raise standards), we take steps in the evaluation of teachers that go in the other direction, toward the routinization and trivialization of teachers' activities *in the classroom*. What is the sense of getting better teachers in the schools if, at the same time, we reduce the intellectual content of the teachers' job?

The performance-based approach to testing teachers can be seen as an intensification of a movement begun in the Progressive Era toward the systematization, or industrialization, of American schooling. In his classic work on educational administration in the Progressive Era, *Education and the Cult of Efficiency,* Raymond E. Callahan chronicled the takeover of the school superintendency by a mindless business efficiency ethic. School administration, instead of emphasizing a quality education, preferred to see things in quantitative terms, emphasizing matters such as budgets, IQ testing, school surveys, and cost accounting while ignoring issues of teaching and learning. Callahan could not argue that the efficiency approach invaded the actual classrooms of the era; that is an achievement reserved for the competency or performance-based education movement of the 1980s.[10]

Because performance-based evaluation predated the 1985 school reform bill, we cannot lay complete responsibility for it at the feet of Georgia's school reformers. We can only say that they will, no doubt, try to intensify the forces already in motion in this area. One change in teaching, however, will be the complete responsibility of the governor and the other reformers: the career ladder. Though the reform bill is vague on what it means by a career ladder, directing the State Board of Education to come up with the same in the near future, there is enough specificity in the purposes given underlying the career ladder to deduce what will be implemented. The career ladder is intended to provide "classroom teachers who demonstrate above average or outstanding competencies relative to teaching skills and their teaching field and exhibit above average or outstanding performance, which may include the achievement of students beyond the level typically expected for their ability, with salary supplements in recognition of such competency and performance."[11] Given what we have here and the operation of career-ladder plans in other states, it seems clear that the career ladder is the latest educational version of a merit-pay plan.

Salary supplements for above-average and outstanding performance seem exactly what would be called for in a merit-pay system. Calling the system a career ladder seems a device to camouflage the obvious with perfumed language. Merit pay has been around in American education since the turn of the twentieth century. The idea first surfaced in big city systems shortly after teacher organizations in those cities forced the school boards to adopt a salary scale and discontinue paying teachers on what the board felt they were worth each year. It ought not to be difficult to understand how the yearly determination of salaries for each teacher was an open invitation to favoritism and corruption. Once a scale was adopted, however, boards often responded with merit-pay plans. In Atlanta in 1915, for example, the board adopted a merit-pay plan ten years after the adoption of a salary scale. Teachers' fears about the unfairness of "merit" were realized when, in the first year of implementation of the merit system, the total school payroll was reduced by $35,000. Similar occurrences in other cities caused teachers and their organizations to recognize merit plans as salary-control plans used to diminish the financial consequences of a salary scale.[12] Is it not likely that one motivation for Georgia's career ladder is to mitigate the consequences of the rather substantial pay raises that are being talked about and have been implemented for teachers recently?

Something very much like the career ladder that is being implemented in Georgia and in other southern states was proposed in the 1960s. Its name, then, was differentiated staffing, and it meant separating teachers into several roles, organizing those roles into a hierarchy, and paying teachers a differential as they rose through the hierarchy. Advocates avoided the label of merit pay, because of teacher opposition, but they noted that what differentiated staffing shared with merit pay was the repudiation of the single-salary scale, which teacher pressure had brought about throughout the country shortly after World

War II. On the single-salary scale, elementary teachers were paid the same as secondary teachers, women the same as men, and blacks the same as whites. Differentiated staffing, if implemented, would have mitigated the financial costs of the single-salary scale. It seems that, at least in some ways, history repeats itself.[13]

In this brief space, I have tried to indicate that there is ample reason to conclude that the recent educational reform thrust in Georgia is anything but a reform. Several significant changes advocated initially were not included in the bill that was signed into law, an obvious nod to political realities. Looking critically at what was passed, with the exception of salary increases for teachers, the student of educational reform is filled with a sense of déjà vu. We've been there before; it wasn't good education then and it isn't now.

On the basis of the criticisms and analysis offered herein, and on my own scholarly work, some indication of my ideas on meaningful educational reform may be pertinent. Let me begin with one suggestion drawn directly from this analysis of the governor's reform bill. It seems that the abolition of vocational education would be a significant and dramatic curriculum change. It would save the schools substantial sums of money, it would reduce a good deal of friction and jealousy among teachers who have seen vocational instructors paid significantly more than regular classroom teachers despite the lack of academic and professional preparation among the vocational teachers, and it would eliminate one of the more blatant ways in which curricular tracking in the schools according to student "interest" makes the schools reproduce the existing social class structure. It would also be an indication that the state wants the schools to take seriously the deficiencies in reading, writing, mathematics, and other basic skills about which we hear so much.

With regard to improving teachers, I see no alternative to the rather humdrum but necessary task of improving their education. This task, of course, starts with their professional education, but it should not be limited to that area. It is difficult to argue that in-service is adequate or that part-time graduate work for teachers is serious. Any professor who faces a class full of teachers in the evening after they have put in a hard day of work and proceeds to "teach" them for three or four hours must understand that a game is being played here. Perhaps the money saved by abolishing vocational education, or by not instituting and maintaining testing programs of enormous size and complexity, could be spent on allowing teachers paid leaves for study, both in professional education and in their academic fields. If we who teach teachers were to be confronted by full-time students, we might be challenged to offer them rigorous courses that, when completed, might mean something to the teachers. In my own graduate course in the history of education (hardly a popular choice for many teachers or their advisers on the education faculty), I have had substantial success by indicating (not that I show what was wrong in their own teaching, but by announcing that I assumed initially that they were competent in their classrooms) that the history of education had some interesting and relevant things to say about the contexts in which they were working, and that they would be evaluated on the basis of how well they could intellectually grapple with the issues and problems presented. If they could not handle ideas in writing or class discussion, I had a reason for doubt about their competence in the classroom and, thus, a low grade indicated both difficulty in graduate school and possible difficulty on the job.

As for preservice education, we in colleges of education have been bombarded with several panaceas like competency-based education in the two decades in which I have been working. As a historian of education, I know that "revolutions" in teacher education have come and gone for at least 140 years. Now we are hearing a lot about 5-year programs in professional education as the answer to our problems. Unless we seriously address the intellectual rigor of our existing course and experiences, what is the use of adding a year to our programs? If we raised the quality of our programs (in standard academic ways) we would go a long way toward raising the self-image of the teachers we produce. Our students know that it's "easy" in education; they hear it from their colleagues and from their instructors in fields outside education. Let's do something about that by making it not easy. Let's challenge our students to produce intellectually. By not challenging them, we open the door for the governor of New Jersey (and officials in other states) to bypass professional education courses in certifying teachers.

My own recommendations are not offered with the expectation that they will revolutionize the schools. That is part of our problem. The schools will not be revolutionized, no matter what we, or politicians, do. Society gets the schools it deserves. Until the citizens of Georgia indicate that they want schools that are intellectually demanding and socially equitable, they will get what they are now getting. Neither the state politicians' program nor the national administration's exhortations are going to alter the situation. They are likely to make it worse.

Part Three

Imagining Sisyphus Happy with Educational Reformers

DAVID E. DENTON

I am addressing the philosopher's role in discussions about educational reform, and I am doing that from a very negative posture. I'm not certain at all that we should even be in that discursive space. To clarify what is meant by "a very negative posture" I shall quickly identify three senses of "reform" and relate those to what Paul Ricoeur calls the philosopher's two vows. Then will come the introduction of Sisyphus, that mythical educator who pushes his rock up the mountain of Hades until, well, at least until retirement. Some educational reformers will come along to help Sisyphus, of course, and while discussing their purported assistance I will set forth my argument, which is a development of the third sense of "reform."

Three Senses of Reform

The first sense of reform is the most common, yet its meaning may be the most hidden. In this sense, reform has reference to methods, strategies, policies, and practices that will enhance, so it is claimed, the efficiency of the educational system by demonstrating, in part, greater productivity with respect to student achievement, defined typically in terms of test scores. Faculty morale, defined in terms of interview and survey data, is considered a consequence of the reform strategies or policies and a contributing variable to the greater productivity. Mapping of this sense of reform in macro and micro levels, and into highly differentiated taxonomies, does not detract from my general characterization.[1] In fact, such refinement of this sense of reform contributes to the masking of its primary assumption, namely, that the system, the machinery itself, lies outside the domain of the problematic. This unquestioned assumption—with its psychological correlate of self-satisfaction—leads to the conclusion that the machinery merely needs a bit more tinkering, perhaps a new microchip in its electronic fuel-injection system.

The second sense of reform is, technically, not a conception of reform at all, but, in the name of reform, it is frequently a call for dismantlement of the system, replacement of existing structures—all implied in some set of a priori assumptions, knowledge of which is perfectly clear to the true believers. Three types of such believers are fairly well known to us: Marxists, religious fundamentalists, and "foundationalist" philosophers. This third type may sound unfamiliar, but think, for a moment, of philosophers of education you have read who have used the a priori assumptions of, say, philosophical idealism as a priori prescriptions for education. For several decades, philosophy of education textbooks have read like works in comparative religion, with varying "-isms" competing for doctrinal superiority, each claiming to be the true foundation of education. My list is not exhaustive; rather, by pointing to Marxists, religious fundamentalists, and foundationalist philosophers, I am attempting to introduce quickly the second sense of reform, which is the predication of change on some set of a priori premises, knowledge of which is clear to the committed ones.

The third sense of the term is less familiar, and much of what follows is an attempted clarification of its meaning. Perhaps it will be sufficient, as an introductory note, to say that this sense is an ontological one. I am using "ontology" in an Heideggerian sense, meaning that it refers to the category of thought about the possible. Much is implied in that, and I shall try to be explicit, in a nontechnical manner, in my use of it.

The Philosopher's Two Vows

Paul Ricoeur wasn't talking about educational reform, but about reform in psychoanalysis and theology, when he paused to remind philosophers in all fields of their two, frequently competing, vows: the Vow of Rigor and the Vow of Obedience.[2] The first, the Vow of Rigor, commits the philosopher to analysis, conceptual clarity, rules of reason, and the like. The Vow of Obedience requires, on the other hand, commitment to a message, presumed to be true, about the present and perhaps also about the future.

Now, and here I go beyond Ricoeur, the problems for the philosopher are two: (1) the consequences of making an exclusive commitment to either vow and (2) the problems entailed in trying to balance them. Both of these bear directly on discourse about educational reform.

If one commits almost exclusively to the Vow of Rigor, then methods of analysis become the defining center of one's work. And when method defines our philosophic work, the result is philosophic methodism. Because I am going to contrast two kinds of -isms, it may help to clarify my meaning of that expression. An -ism is formed when the participants in a sphere of discourse deem that sphere to be self-sufficient with respect to the generation of criteria for judging its worthwhileness. For example, when science judges itself to be independent of external evaluation, it has become not science but scientism. When the point is reached where theory of evolution is used indiscriminately to explain all biological and psychological change, we have evolutionism. Likewise, when method becomes the defining essence of one's work, we have methodism. More technically put, an -ism is a transcendental essence; that is, it is presumed to be transcategorical and logically necessary. In my view, the commitment of Anglo-American philosophy in recent decades has been to the Vow of Rigor, so much so that it is not invalid to characterize it as a methodism.

But what of the consequences when one commits almost exclusively to the Vow of Obedience? Here, too, is an -ism. In philosophy of science, we may speak of it as reductionism, as in, say, the generalization of a single-variable explanation; in literary theory, as synecdoche, as when one reduces that rich history embodied in the concept "law" to the sheriff's patrol car, and says, "Here comes the law"; in moral philosophy, when that enterprise is reduced to certain narrow claims of purity; in theology, when modern reason reduces Aristotle's essentialism to fundamentalism. And, in education, we can speak of back-to-basics. In each case, the consequence is a confident message, however arrived at, a message carrying normative force. For a shorthand, let's call them all fundamentalism.

If I were to stop at this point, the role of the philosopher in respect to educational reform would be rather clear. The one committed to the Vow of Rigor would take his or her methods to the reformer of sense one and assist in clarifying the operations of the system, conducting means-ends analyses, sorting through the theoretical problems of assessment, and, by being a good methodist, contributing to the efficiency and instrumental goals of the state's educational machine. The one committed to the Vow of Obedience would take her or his message to the reformer of sense two and, by pointing out the implications of the fundamental premise, provide rational justification for the greater glory of the revolution.

What I am pointing to, pointedly, is that the first represents method-without-message, or, better, method without awareness of the message, and is the kind of philosophic work compatible with what I see in most of the literature of educational reform. The second represents message-without-method, or, message without awareness of method, and is the kind of philosophic work that would be applauded by those who presume to know the fundamental truth about what ought to be the case in education. There is, however, a third option, the ontological one, and it is not arrived at through some formulaic combining of the two vows; rather, it re-forms "reform."

Reform as an Ontological Term

The language of possibility, what I am calling ontological language, consists primarily of images. There is an ancient tradition for this claim, but it was Heidegger's work on Kant that brought it back into view in this century.[3] Gaston Bachelard, in France, and Edward Casey, in this country, have further developed the argument.[4] In this view, language is considered as openings of possibilities of discourse rather than as univocal concepts. For example, if you were to walk into a class and say, "This is a course in mathematics," you would not be saying what mathematics is, nor would you be predicting all that would take place in the course; rather, by saying, "This is a course in mathematics," you would be opening up possibilities for yourself and your students not to be had were you to say, "This is a course in theater history." Mathematics, in this sense, is an opening of possibilities rather than a sign for substance or function.

Also, while ontological language does not deny the reality and weight of empirical givens, it always points to horizons of possibilities beyond those givens. Heidegger's treatment of temporality, that is, ontological time, and Bachelard's studies of spatiality, ontological space, are the classic developments of this point.[5] But a quick example of spatiality can be done with the room in which you are present. Describing the geometric space of this room would be a straightforward and familiar process. Some might want to include a subjective description, "What does this room feel like?"—a metaphoric language, incidentally. A "description" of the ontological space of this room would include those first descriptions but would go beyond those imagistically. Imagine other uses of this room, say, the annual meeting of the East Arkansas Swingers Association, or a sales display of new casket designs. Imagine this room being much larger, or so small you can carry it out in your pocket. Imagine this room in a state of disrepair, and then watch it being restored. I think you get the point. By multiplying variations, by rotating this room in imaginative space, we begin to appreciate that reform of this room has sources other than data, or definitions, or propositions.

In short, the claim is that ontological language consists of images of possibility and that the direction of those images is toward the future and toward comprehensiveness.

And what of educational reform? It, in my view, is an ontological term. When we speak of reform in this sense, we open ourselves to images of possibilities beyond those to be had by reduction to method or some fundamental "truth"; we attempt to bring images of the future into focus, images of what the adults and the culture of tomorrow might be; and we strive to envision an educational enterprise that is whole and comprehensive. It seems to me that educational reformers, working at whatever level, are after those very things: What is possible beyond the immediate givens? What kind of future do we desire? How can education become whole? But, to repeat, the sources for such reform will be other than data, or definitions, or propositions. A major limit has been in the sense of "reform."

Now, if discourse on educational reform were ontological, what would the philosopher be up to? The answer is: "Much, both exciting and critical." The philosopher might be a leader and stimulator of the dialogue, a clarifier of shared concerns, a connoisseur of images,[6] and yes, an analyzer of fuzzy concepts and logic. In fact, for those primarily interested in analysis, there could be a new era of excitement, for there would be new, richly textured materials on which to use their tools. But, and perhaps more importantly, the philosopher, too, could dream dreams about education's future, could practice what Gaston Bachelard, philosopher of science, called the poetics of reverie.[7]

Imagining Sisyphus Happy

In your reverie, imagine Sisyphus pushing the boulder up to the top and, each time, watching it roll back down. Feel the repetitiveness. Note his mood, his attitude. Camus, in *The Myth of Sisyphus,* identified Sisyphus with the modern worker and ascribed to them both measures of acceptance and irony.[8] For himself, Camus assumed a stoical posture toward Sisyphus's situation. For the reader, he gave an assignment, and with that I think he said more about the limits of his own thought than he was aware. To Sisyphus, he gave irony; to himself, stoicism; to the reader, a command: "One must imagine

Sisyphus happy."[9] That is the last sentence of the book. He asked the reader to do what he, himself, could not: "must imagine"—the necessity of ontological thought.

But let's not close the picture yet. Keep the image of Sisyphus open and watch our reformer-methodist arrive on the scene. Immediately, we have an objective inventory of the setting, analysis of the causal variables, and various prescriptions for the remediation (ugh) of Sisyphus's plight, his plight being the pain of pushing the rock up and the depression of following it down. So, a little biomechanics, a little exercise physiology, a new truss, a B^{12} shot, and a hundred milligrams of Ludiomil four times a day.

Our reformer-fundamentalist arrives on the scene and searches for the most direct way to communicate the messages: Sisyphus, we're going to blow up your rock and the whole damned mountain. Or, Sisyphus, we really need to change your modes of production. Or, Sisyphus, if you would just accept Buddha, Jesus, or Osiris as your lord and savior, all would be peachy-keen. (That's a technical term from the playwright Edward Albee.)

But what do we, of the ontological turn, have to say to Sisyphus? Nothing. Not being experts with methods and "findings," we have nothing to say to him. Nor do we have an a priori message to give him. The distinction is between saying-to and working-with. We can and should work with Sisyphus, first of all, to reestablish that dialogic life that is community. Working with him in this first step is not that of mere facilitation by experts in a group process but the dynamic engagement in conversation and action by those of us who, because of special training and commitment, are known as educators. In the formation of this conversation, this community, Sisyphus brings his past, his present circumstances, and his dreams for the future. And, because genuine dialogue is engagement, we bring ours as well.

Such engagement, such community building, will require—long before we talk explicitly about the forms and practices of schooling—that we learn to use and appreciate the languages of the other. From the other and those with him/her, we may need to learn a local dance; they might even teach us a new hymn or introduce us to their stories of the past and future. From us, being committed educators and not merely expert facilitators, they might learn of the importance of pluralism, of the living reality of different kinds of knowledge, and, maybe, that we also have dreams and images of what might be the case. Sharing our dreams and images, the conversation flows, understandings emerge, and we find ourselves being in community. And we realize that the work-with has begun.

Three actions can now be based on the community's shared images. With Sisyphus, we can position ourselves to be responsive to the possibilities opened to us by our images. (This is the etymological meaning of epistemology. Etymologically, knowledge has to do with our being in an appropriate position; it has no reference at all to verification.) We can then ground our willingness to act toward the future in our shared images. And, third, we can predicate our future actions of reform on the images to which we are committed.[10]

Sisyphus's community begins to formulate, make explicit its images of education, the images on which its members are now willing to ground their future actions. One must not, however, think of those images as only projections of desire, or some other psychological phenomenon, for images are also characterized by structures, some of which are the external, objective variables that constitute, in part, the necessary conditions for making possible the actualization of the images. Material conditions, including structures, systems, and money for actualizing images of reform, are always necessary, even for Sisyphus's community. But, and this the ontological thinker never lets one forget, material conditions are never sufficient. The sufficient conditions for educational reform will come from images had by communities.

One image, a magnificent one, has dominated American conversations about educational reform throughout the century. The image has been that of the Progressivists. They imagined a system of schooling that would be organized on the most sophisticated model of the day; standardized enough so that boys and girls anywhere in the United States would have approximately the same educational opportunities; localized enough to be congruent with the particular histories of different places; and they imagined a common space where all could meet and learn from and appreciate the other. In my view, it was one of the best, and most powerful, images this culture has had. But that image has lost its force. Sisyphus's community no longer finds it an attractive flame; it no longer warms, satisfies, or centers the community's actions. I think I know why. There have been obvious demographic changes; ethnic and religious identities have been recrystallized; and economic conditions have become the source of new anxieties. But I don't think these sorts of considerations fully answer the question of why.

The answer lies in the distinction made between material and sufficient conditions and with the identification of images with sufficient conditions. If the Progressivists' image were still compelling, Sisyphus's community, and others like his, would be willing to commit to it as a guide toward the future even with the demographic and other changes. That image has ceased to be compelling, in major part, because of the actions of educators themselves. Discourse about that image has been reduced to the concepts of bureaucratic regulations, of legal reasoning, of research presuming to be scientific, of professionalization, and to increased centralized (meaning, state) control. The weight of conceptual and legal structures—the reduction to material conditions, in other words—has crushed the image. The successor to the Progressivists' image will emerge when Sisyphus with his community is allowed the space to imagine again. Re-form, new form, will follow.

I leave Sisyphus and the discourse on educational reform with a personal note. Not being a believer in the primacy of the state, I have little interest in finding methods for reforming the existing system of government schools. And, not being a fundamentalist, secular or otherwise, I have no content-filled message for either state-dominated education or Sisyphus. I do have a category of possibility, and, through that, I can imagine Sisyphus happy by letting him return to his own valley, to his own Tennessee River, to make love in his own way, and to educate his children, going with them to whatever their community envisions school to be, vouchers protruding from their pockets.

Democratic Tension and the Future of the Public School

DAVID J. VOLD

Private Enterprise

Society casts its schools in its own image. They reflect its presuppositions and understandings. Moreover, the schools symbolize society's aspirations. Schooling not only constitutes the rite of passage of children into adult society, it represents yet another chance for society to realize its ideals. Given the hope in which the schooling of each new generation is conceived, it is not surprising that its consummation should produce something of a letdown.

While societal disappointment in the schools is nothing new, the current level is particularly strident and widespread. It would appear that popular misgivings about public schools are ripe for exploitation. Americans have witnessed decades of falling test scores coinciding with increased violence in our schools. Moreover, we are beset by the specter of Japanese technological and economic ascendancy—an ascendancy that seems to spell our own decline. The barrage is unrelenting as newspapers and magazines remind us again and again of the woeful ignorance of our youth in such areas as geography, history, mathematics, literature, and the arts. Nor do educational leaders engender confidence for the future. Instead, the strongest voices today belong to the public school critics.

It is particularly significant that the vituperation heaped on public education is largely absent when it comes to private education. In fact, private schooling seems to enjoy broad support across a wide range of political, cultural, and religious boundaries. It is often taken for granted that private schools are superior to public schools and that their mere presence improves public schools through the power of competition.

Advocates of private education tend to adopt one of the following lines of reasoning: either (1) public and private schools have the same goals, but private schools are more effective in reaching them, or (2) education is defined in radically different ways by different people, and the government should not interfere with the educational choices of free people (this might be called the laissez-faire alternative).

Those who hold the first position are often eager to cite statistics on school performance in order to prove their case. Of course, statistics must be interpreted—in other words, they can be misleading—but as long as the proponents of public education and the proponents of private education are disputing the means to the end rather than ends themselves, the issue is addressable. On the other hand, when we cannot even agree about the ends of education, as in the second position, the problem seems insurmountable. This disagreement has led some critics, who otherwise have nothing in common, to advocate doing away with "monolithic" public schooling altogether through the adoption of a voucher system or tuition tax-credit plan. Consider the words of Onalee McGraw: "Given the deep diversity of values and faiths existing in the United States, there is no way that a single, monolithic value-free ethic can be taught without violating the rights of parents to the free exercise of religion and the consequent right to rear their children according to their beliefs."[1] Given the magnitude of the task of reforming the schools, given the fundamentally different understandings of education that are found in society, perhaps our only viable alternative is to turn the schools over to private enterprise and allow individuals to choose whatever education they will.

It is undeniable that "deep diversity of values and faiths" exists in the United States—that is, people approach the world from different perspectives. Such diversity often produces conflict, which, in turn, makes many of us uneasy. Moreover, some conflicts appear to be irresolvable. Therefore, we may attempt to stave them off. One way of warding off conflicts is by isolation: we can avoid those with whom we disagree by establishing a private school. That decision made, the next step is funding—a major problem. Unless we are enormously wealthy, it may be necessary to enlist the help of others, which has often meant trying to secure the support of the government. Of course, the irony is inescapable: seeking government aid for laissez-faire schooling.

Fairness

The most compelling argument for any change in public policy is the invocation of "fairness." If it could be shown that the present system is unfair or that another system is more fair, opposition to change would amount to obstinacy. Fairness, then, is the first plank in the laissez-faire platform.

"How can it be fair," many private school patrons query, "for some people to pay twice for their children's education, while others must pay only once?" We all pay taxes to support the public schools. However, those who make use of them are not required to pay any additional fees to finance the school, while those parents who send their children to private schools must pay tuition in addition to their public school taxes.

Few people can readily afford the expense of private schooling for their children, and even those who can are likely to resent supporting the education of somebody else's child. Add to that number those who have no children, or whose children are past school age or not yet in school, and the level of potential opposition to taxation for public schooling is substantial.

This potential opposition would seem to rest on the twin pillars of "cost" and "parental responsibility." The cost consideration has already been alluded to; the "parental responsibility" argument is directly related to it. Simply stated, this argument holds that parents have the distinct duty of providing for the needs of their own children, but beyond that their duty is nil. Supposedly, society as a whole will flourish as a function of the success of its parts. This principle is at the heart of John Stuart Mill's proposal for education. Mill admonishes: "to bring a child into existence without a fair prospect of being able, not only to provide food for its body, but instruction and training for its mind, is a moral crime, both against the unfortunate offspring and against *society*."[2]

While Mill expresses concern for society, he places the entire weight of responsibility on the individual. This strident individualism may be psychologically appealing, but it is wholly unrealistic. Few babies are the result of long-term budget planning. The only way to be assured that babies will be born only to those who are financially able to provide for all their needs would be through massive sterilization of the poor—an even more repugnant moral crime than saddling society with the care of ill-prepared individuals. Yet, as Mill notes, the actions of individuals have consequences for society; therefore, society has reason to concern itself with the education of each individual child.

Society's stake in the education of each child is substantial and has both positive and negative aspects. From the negative side, an inadequately prepared individual creates a moral, aesthetic, intellectual, and economic drain on the general welfare. From the positive side, a well-prepared individual may help to create a more enlightened, exciting, fulfilling, and prosperous society. The "parental responsibility" argument is too narrow—it inadequately accounts for the legitimate interests of the community in the education of its children. It is the state's interest in the education of all its youth that compels even those citizens who do not directly avail themselves of the public schools to contribute to their support. But even if that is acknowledged, we must still confront the problem of balancing the public welfare with the rights of individual families.

Authority

The task of balancing the sometimes competing interests of the state and the family (or individual) is largely an issue of authority. The state has powerful claims on authority, but, in our society, the same may be said for individuals. It might even be argued that the state's interests are best served when each individual enjoys the greatest possible freedom. Yet, howsoever we may be moved by such rhetoric, we are left with determining just what "the greatest possible freedom" is, that is, where the locus of authority belongs.

Before attacking such a thorny issue, we should be clear that it is relevant to the specific task of educating the young. After all, if the children are adequately educated, what does it matter by whose authority they are educated? If the children learn how to read, write, and do arithmetic, why should it matter whether the state has sanctioned either the school in which they learn or their teachers? Moreover, if, on average, the students at uncertified private schools are performing at a higher level than their counterparts at certified public schools, as measured by standardized tests, is it not the height of presumptuousness to strike the balance of authority on the side of the state? As disturbing as these questions are, they ignore the problem inherent in the term "adequate education."

"Adequate education" is a perceptual problem. Its meaning is dependent on the presuppositions of the inquirer; that is, what one takes to be an adequate education reflects one's prior assumptions—including where one locates authority. Inasmuch as perceptions of "adequate education" vary according to the location of authority, to try to determine the proper location of authority based on one's perception of "adequate education" begs the question.

Here we are confronted with a wide range of alternatives. The state and the individual may agree that skill in reading, writing, and arithmetic is necessary to a good education, yet they may be at odds as to what is sufficient. As Elliot Eisner notes: "What, for example, do we mean by learning to read? Do we mean the ability to read literature or simply to read utility bills? Do we want children to read 'between the lines,' to grasp the meaning of metaphor and connotation, or are we simply interested in decoding? Is wanting to read as important as being able to read?"[3] Parents and the state may be at even greater odds over the role of the school in the interpretation of data and the resolution of problems. Given that both the individual and society have a stake in the education of their children, how are disagreements between them to be resolved?

Should the public schools teach at the level of the lowest common denominator (i.e., should they teach only what all agree is necessary)? Are the schools obligated to provide a "good" education or merely an "adequate" one? How does one determine what is adequate? If parents choose to educate their children in a way that is socially corrupt or perverse, has society the right to protect itself and "its" children? Going beyond the passive role of protection, does the state have the right to take an active role in the inculcation of certain socially popular values in school, for example, competitiveness, consumerism, capitalism, individualism, collectivism, or what have you? The task of identifying socially popular values that might be instilled in the schools is relatively easy. But, while the state might identify the development of one or more of these attitudes as an integral part of an adequate education, an individual family might view the state-endorsed value as miseducative. Of course, there is an escape valve. Those who disapprove of the public schools are free to send their children to private schools.

The right to private schooling was established in *Pierce v. Society of Sisters* in 1925. This case grew out of an Oregon law requiring all children to attend public schools. The Supreme Court overruled the law, declaring, "'the child . . . is not the mere creature of the state.'"[4] The Court viewed the Oregon law as amounting to an unconstitutional attempt to standardize its children.

In examining this and subsequent cases, Stephen Arons has concluded that, far more than an escape hatch for parents who object to public schooling, the *Pierce* decision makes public schooling virtually untenable. Specifically, Arons argues that (1) because education—public or private—must take place within a social context, socialization cannot be avoided; (2) within a public school context, socialization amounts to the inculcation of majority values; (3) the First Amendment does not allow the government to inculcate beliefs or ideologies even when they are endorsed by the majority; (4) therefore, parents who choose free schooling are forced to sacrifice their First Amendment rights; and (5) poor parents, who cannot afford the choice, must accept state-sponsored socialization of their children.[5] Arons identifies two ways to circumvent this dilemma. The state (at great expense) might provide a full range of alternative schools, each with a different social environment, from which the parents could choose. Or the state could get out of the school business (or at least change its role from teacher to benefactor). That is, the state could, in effect, provide all parents with a specific amount of money for each child and allow the parents to select whatever school they will—a voucher plan—or return to them a reasonable portion of their tuition in the form of a tuition tax credit (philosophically identical to the voucher plan).

No one can predict the practical consequences of establishing a voucher-type system. However, it is reasonable to expect that some parents whose children are currently in public schools would choose private schooling for their children if they could afford to do so. In other words, cost is an important (albeit not the only) factor in the parental decision concerning whether to send one's children to a public or private school. As the voucher plan would reduce the cost factor, it can be anticipated that the private schools would benefit—perhaps to the eventual elimination of the public school system. Given the assurance of sufficient funds—expended at the discretion of individual families—a voucher system would probably encourage the mushrooming of private schools, at least some of which would pander to the ideological prejudices of some parents, with the result that some (perhaps many) of the children would be indoctrinated along narrow—even antisocial—lines. Cost, then, serves as a safeguard, not only for the continuance of the public school system but also against rampant individualism and social division. The argument that would have us put these considerations aside has, once again, to do with fairness, but this time it is "fairness to the poor."

The fairness argument holds that no one's constitutional rights should be abridged because of his or her financial status.

Arons contends that the "right" of the poor to send their children to private schools (established by *Pierce*) is rendered meaningless due to the cost of tuition, while the same right for the wealthy is undiminished. In short, the present system is said to victimize the poor. Thus, fairness would seem to require the state to provide rich and poor alike with educational vouchers.

While Arons's argument has won the support of many, it does not ring true. Its chief weakness is its highly questionable leap from the mere fact of socialization to the assertion of an unconstitutional inculcation of majority values. If one were to take Arons seriously, virtually all public forms of social interaction would constitute a violation of the First Amendment. Arons is correct, however, in his assessment that a voucher system would lead to the end of public schooling, though not because the public schools violate the First Amendment or because of the greater popularity of private schooling.

If it is unfair for one individual to pay for the education of somebody else's child, then only those who avail themselves of the public schools should pay the taxes to support them. But if only those whose children attend public schools pay taxes to support them, then the tax is really a form of tuition. If parents are paying tuition to send their children to public school, then public school is really private school. Therefore, if one accepts the argument that it is not fair that parents should be expected to pay a school tax if they are also paying tuition to send their own children to private school (the so-called double taxation issue) or that it is not fair that people should have to pay a school tax if they have no children, then, it follows that the public school ceases to exist; that is, it has become a private school by definition. Of course supporters of the public school contend that even those who do not have children in the public school "use" it—it benefits each of us to live in an educated society. Moreover, it appears naive to believe that the poor would be significantly better educated if they attended private schools or that exclusive private schools would even let in more than a handful of the poor.

In the final analysis, the issue comes down to what is in the public welfare. Few people would deny that parents ought to have the option to send their children to a private school, but should that option exist at the expense of a public school?

One of the few common elements that most of our people share is public schooling. Whatever objections to public schooling one might have, it has greater potential for serving the common good than private schooling, which, on the contrary, is likely to exacerbate social diversities. While a certain amount of diversity can strengthen a society, it can also produce social disintegration. We do not know what the optimal amount of diversity is, but once that level is exceeded we may be unable to regain what is lost. We cannot afford to set social policy by trial and error any more than we can allow a surgeon to operate by that same method.

The Interest of the State

Much has been made of the individual family's rights, vis-à-vis those of the state, in the selection of an acceptable educational environment, and in our society those rights are essential—history is rife with examples of totalitarian states where such rights are nonexistent. Moreover, society is the ultimate beneficiary when individuals are free to criticize the policies of the state. At the same time, in a democratic society, the state is the composite of the individuals within it. Surely, the private rights of individuals are not diminished when they are collectively held. We should be mindful of the dangers of compulsory unification of opinion, but that is not to suggest that unity is undesirable—quite the contrary. Of course, "unity" can be abused. Atrocities can be committed in the name of "the people" or for "the general good." However, that a slogan, such as "the good of the state," may be invoked to justify evil acts does not prove that the state's interests should be secondary any more than evil performed in the name of religion should lead to a condemnation of religion.

The fact that "the good of the state" can be misused to defend an evil act points to our common recognition that what is good for the state is, in fact, good. The critical concern is the consequence of an act—the end does justify the means unless the means subverts the intended end. If an act is evil, it is reasonable to assume that the consequences for the state will be evil regardless of whether those who advocate the evil action try to pass it off as good for the state. When Hitler orders the murder of Jews "for the good of the state," it does not follow that the good of the state is unimportant. Rather, what is rejected is Hitler's perception of what is good for the state. Of course, the majority within a society may be as mistaken as the single individual in its perception of what is in the interest of the state. However, given constitutional safeguards, that is the risk inherent within a democracy.

It is democracy, Arons charges, that is violated by the public school system in the United States today. Democracy vests sovereignty in the people—each individual (in concert with the others) is supposed to be free to direct his or her own destiny *and that of the state*—yet school policy is set by the state and individuals often feel excluded from the process. Because the state is amorphous, its tasks are carried out by its bureaucracy. Bureaucracy results in the domination of society by experts, both in developing policy and in its implementation. Consequently, school policy may not be based on local values but on established educational theory. Arons and McGraw denounce bureaucracy as imposing the values of the education establishment on the people. In short, they insist that leaving educational decisions to educational experts is, as McGraw has put it, "inconsistent with the democratic premises of our society."[6] The education establishment likes to counter that, in the interest of democracy, educational policy cannot be left to the petty politics and provincialism of local communities.

In a paper entitled "Censorship, Academic Freedom, and the Public School Teacher," Michael Littleford argues that the defense of democracy rests not with the public but with the class of professional educators. While she urges respect toward the "enemies" of democracy (i.e., "the frustrated elements of the lower middle class who are not sure why they are so angry at educators and schools"), she cautions professional educators to be "firm in defense of democratic ideals."[7]

Littleford's position seems to be that the public schools are *for* the public but not *of* the public. Apparently, the public cannot be trusted to act in its own best interest. Therefore, the professional educator serves the public by protecting the democratic ideals that the public is in danger of discarding. But how does a bureaucracy safeguard democracy when it denies in its actions the very sovereignty of the people that it affirms in its words? The rise of the professional education bureaucracy inevitably diminishes the role of the community in the school.

The drive toward centralization of authority in education began in the 1830s with the rise of the Common School movement. This reform movement urged the establishment of compulsory schooling under the control of a trained teaching staff. Its purpose was moral and political. The motivation for common school reform sprang from the desire to inculcate proper values (the values of the middle class) in the children of the immigrants and other poor people and to stave off the growing social influence of the common folk.[8] The key to this effort was the centralization of authority, that is, wresting the decision-making function from the local communities and putting it in the hands of an elite state board.

While the Common School reformers of the nineteenth century were unable to eradicate local control, their twentieth-century heirs were more successful in that regard. With the emergence of the Progressive movement in education and the rise of the corporate model, school districts consolidated on a large scale. The movement toward consolidation, centralization, and efficient administration has produced a school significantly unlike that which existed previously. Centralized and consolidated schools appear better equipped to keep society on the competitive edge within a complex, technological world. They also increase the social distance between the community and its schools. This distancing is illustrated in the evolution of the local school board.

At the same time that the districts were getting larger, school boards were getting smaller. Cities that had once had dozens of local boards, with hundreds of members, soon had a single board with fewer than a dozen members. As the representation of the citizens diminished in number, it also diminished in kind. Whereas local (ward) board members resembled their constituents socially and economically (and, one might add, ethnically, religiously, etc.), centralization produced a school board whose members (whether appointed or elected) were apt to contrast with the population they supposedly represented.[9]

It might appear that citizens had reason for concern as they began to lose control of the schools to remote boards and professional bureaucrats. Nevertheless, they were reassured by the oft-repeated slogan, "The schools must teach children how to think, not what to think." If the schools were not going to teach any values, what was there to worry about? Of course, some worried that the schools were creating a moral vacuum. And, while that is impossible—it is impossible to think without thinking about something—it may be that the schools have less influence for good than they ought to have.

Centralization of authority within the school system may help to stabilize a large society, but it is not an unmixed blessing for a democracy. *Society* requires unity, *democracy* encourages diversity. A *democratic society* sustains itself as its members participate in their government and share a common commitment to the good of the whole. Nowhere is the government closer to the people than in the public schools. However, centralization, with its concomitant bureaucratization, has largely removed the government of the schools from the people. The voucher plan would restore the democratic right of choice to the individual families by replacing the public schools with a decentralized private school system, but this option seems to come at the expense of social unity. Is there an alternative?

If a highly centralized public school system diminishes democracy and a decentralized private school system diminishes social unity, perhaps an acceptable alternative might be found in a decentralized public school system. Such a system might fulfill the needs of society without sacrificing the principles of democracy. Because it would be decentralized, one might anticipate local support and participation. Because it would be public, its emphasis would not be on exclusivity, ideological or otherwise. By encouraging widespread citizen participation, it could offer the communities that make up our society a higher degree of autonomy. Also, it could provide the thread of continuity—shared commitment to the democratic process and the common good—that the society as a whole requires. Moreover, if community members were to have a realistic expectation of influencing policy, the level of involvement would likely increase. It is possible that such involvement could result in social disintegration as conflicting interests clash, but it is at least as likely that conflicting interests would reach conclusions that are workable, thereby reinforcing the unity that is fundamental in society.

It is possible that given greater public control of the public schools, the education offered in some communities would become more provincial than at present. It is even possible that our society as a whole would be rendered less able to compete with other technological giants. That is a risk we may wish to minimize. It is a risk that can be eliminated by fiat in a centralized system or by persuasion in one that is decentralized. Nevertheless, democracy does not guarantee preeminence to a nation but sovereignty to the people.

Notes

Introduction

1. Charles A. Brown, "Only School Users Should Pay For Them," *Tuscaloosa News,* 18 Oct. 1987, sec. A.

2. Elliot W. Eisner, *The Educational Imagination: On the Design and Evaluation of School Programs* (New York: Macmillan, 1985), 2.

3. Paul E. Peterson, "Did the Education Commissions Say Anything?" *Brookings Review* 2 (1983):4.

4. Thomas S. Popkewitz, "Organization and Power: Teacher Education Reforms," *Social Education* 51 (1987):500.

5. Paul Brandwein, *Memorandum: On Renewing Schooling and Education* (New York: Harcourt Brace Jovanovich, 1981).

6. A. Harry Passow, "Tackling the Reform Reports of the 1980s," *Phi Delta Kappan* 65 (June 1984):683.

7. Catherine Cornbleth, "Knowledge in Curriculum and Teacher Education," *Social Education* 51 (1987):514.

8. Gerald R. Gill, *Meanness Mania: The Changed Mood* (Washington, D.C.: Howard University Press, 1980).

9. Joseph L. DeVitis, "State Education Reforms Lower Morale," *Jackson* (Tennessee) *Sun,* 15 Feb. 1987, sec. E.

10. Willis D. Hawley, "Toward a Comprehensive Strategy for Addressing the Teacher Shortage," *Phi Delta Kappan* 67 (June 1986):712–18.

Public Education's Last Hurrah?

1. Fred M. Wirt, "National Australia–United States Education: A Commentary," in *Educational Policy in Australia and America: Comparative Perspectives,* ed. William Lowe Boyd and D. Smart (New York: Falmer Press, 1987).

2. Allan Odden, "Education Finance 1985: A Rising Tide or Steady Fiscal State?" *Educational Evaluation and Policy Analysis* 7, no. 4 (1985):395–407.

3. D. Boaz, ed., *Left, Right and Babyboom: America's New Politics* (Washington, D.C.: CATO Institute, 1986), 34.

4. Paul E. Peterson, "Economic and Political Trends Affecting Education" (Paper presented at the Brookings Institution, Washington, D.C., n.d.).

5. Paul E. Peterson, *The Politics of School Reform, 1870–1940* (Chicago: University of Chicago Press, 1985).

6. F. E. Emery and E. L. Trist, "The Causal Texture of Organizational Environments," *Human Relations* 18 (1965):21–32.

7. Albert Shanker, "The First Real Crisis," in *Handbook of Teaching and Policy,* ed. Lee S. Shulman and G. Sykes (New York: Longman, 1983).

8. D. L. Clark and T. A. Astuto, "The Significance and Permanence of Changes in Federal Education Policy," *Educational Researcher* 15, no. 8 (1986):4–13.

9. M. W. Kirst and W. I. Garms, "The Political Environment of School Finance Policy in the 1980s," in *School Finance Policies and Practices—The 1980s: A Decade of Conflict,* ed. James W. Guthrie (Cambridge, Mass.: Ballinger, 1980).

10. J. V. Baldridge and T. Deal, eds., *The Dynamics of Organizational Change in Education* (Berkeley, Calif.: McCutchan, 1983).

11. William Lowe Boyd, "Local Influences on Education," *Encyclopedia of Educational Research,* 5th ed. (New York: Macmillan and Free Press, 1982), 118–29.

12. M. W. Kirst, "Curricular Leadership at the State Level: What Is the New Focus?" *NASSP Bulletin* (Apr. 1987):8–14.

13. D. Mann, ed., *Making Change Happen?* (New York: Teachers College Press, 1978).

14. R. F. Elmore, "Complexity and Control: What Legislators and Administrators Can Do about Implementing Public Policy," in Shulman and Sykes, *Handbook of Teaching and Policy.*

15. D. Plank, "The Ayes of Texas: Rhetoric, Reality, and School Reform," *Politics of Education Bulletin* 13, no. 2 (1986):13–16.

16. S. M. Johnson, "Incentives for Teachers: What Motivates, What Matters," *Educational Administration Quarterly* 22, no. 3 (1986): 54–79.

17. James W. Guthrie, "School-Based Management: The Next Needed Education Reform," *Phil Delta Kappan* 68 (Dec. 1986):306.

18. Paula F. Silver, "Review of *Organizational Environments: Ritual and Rationality,*" *Educational Administration Quarterly* 22, no. 2 (1986):140. (Emphasis added.)

19. Ibid., 141.

20. Kirst, "Curricular Leadership," 8–14.

21. P. G. Altbach, G. P. Kelly, and L. Weis, eds., *Excellence in Education: Perspectives on Policy and Practice* (Buffalo: Prometheus Books, 1985).

22. Allan Odden, "When Votes and Dollars Mingle: A First Analysis of State Reforms," *Politics of Education Bulletin* 13, no. 2 (1986):6.

23. Plank, "Ayes of Texas," 13.

24. "Teachers Found Skeptical about Impact of Reforms," *Education Week,* 19 Nov. 1986, 6, 18.

25. M. Levary, "Few Teachers Back Career Ladder, Survey Says," *Knoxville News-Sentinel,* 25 Feb. 1986, sec. A.

26. B. Malen and A. W. Hart, "Career Ladder Reform: A Multilevel Analysis of Initial Efforts," *Educational Evaluation and Policy Analysis* 9, no. 1 (1987):9–23. (Emphasis added.)

27. Ibid., 20.

28. Arthur E. Wise, *Legislated Learning: The Bureaucratization of the American Classroom* (Berkeley and Los Angeles: University of California Press, 1979).

29. J. Evangelauf, "School-Reform Movement Said to Be Moving from Capitols to Classrooms," *Chronicle of Higher Education,* 7 May 1986, 22.

30. David Tyack, *The One Best System* (Cambridge: Harvard University Press, 1974).

31. R. K. Jung and M. W. Kirst, "Beyond Mutual Adaptation, Into the Bully Pulpit: Recent Research on the Federal Role in Education," *Educational Administration Quarterly* 22, no. 3 (1986):80–109.

32. R. Weatherley and M. Lipsky, "Street-Level Bureaucrats and Institutional Innovation: Implementing Special-Education Reform," *Harvard Educational Review* 47, no. 2 (May 1977):171–97.

33. L. M. McNeil, "Exit, Voice and Community: Magnet Teachers' Responses to Standardization" (Paper presented at American Educational Research Association annual meeting, San Francisco, Apr. 1986).

34. T. J. Peters and R. H. Waterman, Jr., *In Search of Excellence: Lessons from America's Best-Run Companies* (New York: Harper and Row, 1982), 15, 318.

35. E. H. Schein, *Organizational Psychology* (Englewood Cliffs, N.J.: Prentice-Hall, 1965).

36. Elmore, "Complexity and Control."

37. Ibid., 358.

38. Paul E. Peterson, *City Limits* (Chicago: University of Chicago Press, 1981).

39. B. R. Clark, "The High School and the University: What Went Wrong in America, Part I," *Phi Delta Kappan* 66 (Feb. 1985):391–97; and "The High School and the University: What Went Wrong in America, Part II," *Phi Delta Kappan* 66 (Mar. 1985):472–75.

40. Albert H. Quie, "More 'Choice' Is Key to Public-School Reform," *Education Week,* 20 May 1987, 19.

41. K. D. Peterson, J. Murphy, and P. Hallinger, "Superintendents' Perceptions of the Control and Coordination of the Technical Core in Effective School Districts," *Educational Administration Quarterly* 23, no. 1 (1987):79–95.

42. J. G. March and J. P. Olsen, "Organizing Political Life: What Administration Reorganization Tells Us about Government," *American Political Science Review* 22 (June 1983):288.

Bill Clinton and Arkansas

1. Bill Clinton, "Who Will Manage the Schools?" *Phi Delta Kappan* 68 (Nov. 1986):208.

2. Bill Clinton, "We've Made Progress in Education, but the Job Isn't Over," *Arkansas Gazette,* 13 Dec. 1987, sec. A.

3. Sara Murphy, ed., *Fulfilling the Promise of Reform: Arkansas Reform Study, 1985–88* (Little Rock: Winthrop Rockefeller Foundation, Dec. 1988), esp. 3, 6, 10–11, 19, 22, 28, 47, and 56.

4. Ibid., 46.

5. Ibid., 7, 36.

6. Ibid., 7–8, 31–38.

7. Ibid., 38.

8. Ibid., 31.

9. Dr. Sara Murphy, interview with the author, Little Rock, 27 Nov. 1989.

10. Murphy, *Fulfilling the Promise of Reform,* 38–39.

11. Ibid., 11, 23, 27–28, 37–38, 54.

12. S. B. Sarason, *The Culture of the School and the Problem of Chance,* 2d ed. (Boston: Allyn and Bacon, 1982); and Barbara B. Tye, *Multiple Realities: A Study of 13 American High Schools* (Lanham, Md.: University Press of America, 1985).

13. J. S. Bruner, "Learning and Thinking," in *Readings in the Psychology of Cognition,* ed. R. C. Anderson and D. P. Ausubel (New York: Holt, Rinehart and Winston, 1965), 77.

14. T. Corcoran and B. Wilson, *The Search for Successful Second-*

ary Schools: The First Three Years of the Secondary School Recognition Program (Philadelphia: Research for Better Schools, Oct. 1986); and S. L. Lightfoot, *The Good High School: Portraits of Character and Culture* (New York: Basic Books, 1983).

15. Allan Odden and B. Anderson, "How Successful State Education Improvement Programs Work," *Phi Delta Kappan* 67 (Apr. 1986):582–85.

16. Tye, *Multiple Realities,* 371–75.

17. Bruner, "Learning and Thinking," 77.

18. Lightfoot, *Good High School;* and Corcoran and Wilson, *Search.*

19. M. Rutter, et al., *Fifteen Thousand Hours: Secondary Schools and Their Effects on Children* (Cambridge: Harvard University Press, 1979), 190–94.

20. Murphy, *Fulfilling the Promise of Reform,* 41–42.

21. William W. Wayson, *Up from Excellence: The Impact of the Excellence Movement on Schools* (Bloomington, Ind.: Phi Delta Kappa Educational Foundation, 1986), 11–13.

22. Odden and Anderson, "How Successful State Education Improvement Programs Work," 582–83. Also see T. B. Timar and D. L. Kirp, "Education Reform in the 1980s: Lessons from the States," *Phi Delta Kappan* 70 (Mar. 1989):504–11.

23. Arthur E. Wise, "Legislated Learning Revisited," *Phi Delta Kappan* 69 (Jan. 1988):329–30.

24. Clinton, "We've Made Progress."

25. Marcus Aurelius, *Meditations,* in vol. 12 of *Great Books of the Western World,* ed. Robert Hutchins (Chicago: Encyclopedia Britannica, 1952), 279, 282.

26. M. W. Kirst, *Who Controls Our Schools? American Values in Conflict* (Stanford: Stanford Alumni Association, 1984), 7–19; and Tye, *Multiple Realities,* 371–75.

27. T. B. Gregory and G. R. Smith, *High Schools as Communities: The Small School Reconsidered* (Bloomington, Ind.: Phi Delta Kappa Educational Foundation, 1987).

28. Ralph W. Tyler, "Education Reforms," *Phi Delta Kappan* 69 (Dec. 1987):279; and Barbara B. Tye, "The Deep Structure of Schooling," *Phi Delta Kappan* 69 (Dec. 1987):283.

Curriculum Reform & Professional Expertise

1. Marshall A. Harris, "Memorandum to Members of the Florida Education Council," Tallahassee: Florida Department of Education, 20 June 1984.

2. Ibid., 3–6.

3. *Florida School Laws, 1985 Edition,* s. 232.246, Tallahassee: Florida State Archives, 111.

4. Ibid., s. 232.2454, pp. 110–11.

5. Ibid.

6. Ibid.

7. Ibid., s. 233.011, pp. 120–21.

8. Ibid.

9. Ibid., s. 233.09, pp. 130–31.

10. Local districts are allowed to spend up to 50 percent of the annual state allocation of funds for instructional materials for materials that are not on the state list.

11. Lee S. Shulman, "Knowledge and Teaching: Foundations of the New Reform," *Harvard Educational Review* 57, no. 1 (Feb. 1987):12.

12. Ernest L. Boyer, *Teacher Involvement in Decisionmaking: A State-by-State Profile* (Washington, D.C.: Carnegie Foundation for the Advancement of Teaching, Sept. 1988).

13. Ibid., 2–3.

14. Teachers' certification must now be renewed every five years; and "professional service contracts" for teachers do not provide lifetime tenure—they too must be renewed.

Merit Pay: An Unworkable Past

1. Peter F. Drucker, *The Practice of Management* (New York: Harper and Brothers, 1954).

2. "Teacher Evaluations Need to Be Custom Made," *Phi Delta Kappan* 68 (Jan. 1987):408–09.

3. Drucker, *Practice of Management,* 329–38.

4. *State Model for Local Evaluation* (Nashville: State Department of Education, n.d.).

5. William C. Bagley, *Classroom Management: Its Principles and Technique* (New York: Macmillan, 1908). Chap. 18 is entitled "The Ethics of Schoolcraft."

Educational Reform in Mississippi

1. Mary F. Sumners, "Education in Ante-bellum Tishomingo County," *Journal of Mississippi History* 20 (Jan.–Oct. 1958):229. See also Edward Mayes, *History of Education in Mississippi* (Washington, D.C.: United States Bureau of Education, 1899); and William D. Mc-

Cain, "Education in Mississippi in 1860," *Journal of Mississippi History* 22 (Jan.–Oct. 1960):155.

2. McCain, "Education in Mississippi," 156.

3. Jim B. Pearson and Edgar Fuller, *Education in the States: Historical Development and Outlook* (Washington, D.C.: National Education Association of the United States, 1969), 649.

4. Stuart G. Noble, *Forty Years of the Public Schools in Mississippi* (1918; reprint, New York: AMS Press, 1972), 9.

5. Ibid., 11.

6. *A Compilation of the Constitutional Provisions and Legislative Acts Pertaining to the Common Schools in the State of Mississippi* (Jackson: Power and Barksdale, 1876), 9–23; and Pearson and Fuller, *Education in the States,* 650, 676. It should be noted that there is a discrepancy between these two sources indicating the minimum number of inhabitants needed for incorporated municipalities to establish separate school systems.

7. Pearson and Fuller, *Education in the States,* 651.

8. Noble, *Forty Years of the Public Schools,* 70.

9. Ibid.

10. Ibid., 71.

11. Pearson and Fuller, *Education in the States,* 652.

12. Ibid., 653.

13. Kern Alexander and Kenneth Forbis Jordan, *Legal Aspects of Educational Choice: Compulsory Attendance and Student Assignment* (Topeka: National Organization on Legal Problems of Education, 1973), 9.

14. Mississippi State Department of Education, *Biennial Report and Recommendations of the State Superintendent, 1915–16* (Jackson: State Department of Education, 1916), 5.

15. William A. Person and Robert L. Jenkins, "A Documentary and Interpretive History of Compulsory School Attendance Laws in Mississippi: A Preliminary Report" (Paper presented at the 1984 annual conference of the Southeastern Regional Association of Teacher Educators, Williamsburg, Va., Nov. 1984).

16. William H. Hand, *The Need of Compulsory Education in the South* (Washington, D.C.: United States Bureau of Education Bulletin, No. 2, 1914), 101.

17. *General Laws of the State of Mississippi* (1918), chap. 258.

18. Mississippi State Department of Education, *Biennial Report and Recommendations of the State Superintendent, 1920–21* (Jackson: State Department of Education, 1921), 11. These counties included Claiborne, Jefferson, Franklin, and Wilkinson. The primary concern

expressed by the voters in these counties was that the large black student population would claim most of the school tax dollars (provided in a larger proportion by the white taxpayers) due to the enforcement of House Bill No. 177.

19. Although one of the South's most recognizable progressive governors, Vardaman, affectionately known as the "White Chief" by his supporters, was perhaps the region's most notable racist. His white supremacist views carried him to gubernatorial victory in 1903 and included opposition to black "literary education" in Mississippi because it only "ruined a good field hand." For an account of Vardaman's views on black education, see William F. Holmes, *The White Chief: James Kimble Vardaman* (Baton Rouge: Louisiana State University Press, 1970).

20. Department of Education, *Biennial Report, 1920–21*, 9; and Mississippi State Department of Education, *Biennial Report, 1924–25* (Jackson: State Department of Education, 1925), 9.

21. Pearson and Fuller, *Education in the States,* 655.

22. Mississippi State Department of Education, *A Compilation of the School Laws of Mississippi* (Jackson: State of Mississippi, Department of Education, 1958), 385–94.

23. Pearson and Fuller, *Education in the States,* 657.

24. Mississippi State Department of Education, *Biennial Report, 1965–67* (Jackson: State Department of Education, 1967), 25–26.

25. Public Education Study Committee, *A Study of Critical Issues in Mississippi's Public Schools with Recommendations and Legislative Proposals for Improving the Public Educational System in the State (Summary Report)* (Jackson: State of Mississippi, 1973).

26. *Booz-Allen & Hamilton Report, Summary of State-Wide Education Study, Phase I, State of Mississippi* (Jackson: State of Mississippi, 1967).

27. Ibid. See "Letter of Transmittal" by Governor Paul B. Johnson in the front of the document, dated 10 Mar. 1967.

28. John Ray Skates, *Mississippi, A Bicentennial History* (New York: Norton Press, 1979), 166–67.

29. Edward N. Akin, *Mississippi, An Illustrated History* (Northridge Calif.: Windsor Publications, 1987), 124.

30. *Memphis Commercial Appeal,* 1 Aug. 1979.

31. *Memphis Commercial Appeal,* 13 Nov. 1982; and *Columbus Commercial Dispatch,* 7 Apr. 1982.

32. *Jackson Clarion-Ledger,* 24 Oct. 1982.

33. *Starkville Daily News,* 25 Oct. 1982.

34. *Jackson Clarion-Ledger,* 7 Dec. 1982.

35. *Jackson Clarion-Ledger,* 24 Oct. 1982.

36. *Memphis Commercial Appeal,* 4 Dec. 1982.

37. *Meridian Star,* 4 Sept. 1983.

38. Ron Brownlee, "Applying a New Federalism Solution to the Problem of Educational Deprivation: An Assessment of the Implementation of Mississippi's 1982 Education Reform Act" (Mississippi State University Library, Special Collections, n.d.), 2. Shortly after the initial reorganization, two additional districts were added to bring the total to 153.

39. *Columbus Commercial Dispatch,* 5 Sept. 1984.

40. *Jackson Clarion-Ledger,* 5 May 1985.

41. *Jackson Clarion-Ledger,* 18 Nov. 1983.

42. Ibid.

43. *Starkville Daily News,* 4 May 1985.

44. Mississippi State Legislature, "House Bill No. 4," sec. 12, p. 11.

45. Mississippi State Department of Education, *Five-Year Plan for Educational Improvement, Support Document, 1986–1990* (Jackson: State Department of Education, 1986), III-14. Actually, three types of consolidated districts are possible under current law: regular, line, and interstate line. Regular consolidated districts lie within a single county, line consolidated districts embrace territory in more than one county, and interstate line districts would include territory both in Mississippi and in an adjoining county of a bordering state.

46. Ibid., III-15.

47. *Jackson Clarion-Ledger,* 14 July 1985; and Department of Education, *Five-Year Plan, 1986–1990,* III-17.

48. *Mississippi Code, 1972, Annotated Cumulative Supplement,* sec. 37-57-105, 37-57-107.

49. *Jackson Clarion-Ledger,* 14 July 1985.

50. Ibid.

51. Department of Education, *Five-Year Plan, 1986–1990,* III-17.

52. *Jackson Clarion-Ledger,* 14 July 1985.

53. *Jackson Clarion-Ledger,* 20 Nov. 1984.

54. *General Laws of the State of Mississippi* (1977), chap. 483.

55. William Winter, "Speech to the Mississippi Economic Council, 13 May 1981," Governor's Papers Record Group 27, Box 1314, Mississippi Department of Archives and History, Jackson.

56. *Jackson Clarion-Ledger,* 28 Nov. 1982.

57. Department of Education, *Five-Year Plan, 1986–1990,* III-74.

58. Winter, "Speech to the Mississippi Economic Council."

59. State Legislature, "House Bill No. 4," sec. 21, pp. 2, 5, 6, 7, 8.

60. Department of Education, *Five-Year Plan, 1986–1990,* III-74.

61. Ibid.

62. *Jackson Clarion-Ledger,* 28 Apr. 1984.

63. "The Mississippi Reform Act Five Years Later, A Report to the People of Mississippi from Dr. Richard A. Boyd, State Superintendent of Education" (Jackson: State Department of Education, 1987), 22; and *Mississippi Code, 1972, Annotated,* sec. 37-13-91, p. 2.

64. "Mississippi Reform Act Five Years Later," 22.

65. Mississippi State Department of Education, "School Dropouts by Reason, 1987–1988" (Jackson: State Department of Education, n.d.), 57.

66. *Mississippi Code, 1972, Annotated,* sec. 37-16-1, 37-16-3, 37-16-5, 37-16-7, 37-16-9; and Department of Education, *Five Year Plan, 1986–1990,* II-8. Mississippi already had a statewide testing program. Assessment testing under the Education Reform Act, however, specifically mandated testing in grades different from those usually tested in the state.

67. *Mississippi Code, 1972, Annotated,* sec. 37-16-7.

68. Mississippi State Department of Education, "1985–1986 School Year Report on BSAP, FLE, ACT for Mississippi" (Jackson: State Department of Education, n.d.), 3–6.

69. Ibid., 7–8.

70. Mississippi State Department of Education, *Mississippi State-wide Testing: Pupil Performance, 1988* (Jackson: State Department of Education, 1988), 73–75.

71. Mississippi State Department of Education, "Mississippi School District Profile, 1987–88, Lowndes County School District" (Jackson: State Department of Education, 1988).

72. *Columbus Commercial Dispatch,* 1 Mar. 1982.

73. *Jackson Clarion-Ledger,* 3 Jan. 1983.

74. *Jackson Clarion-Ledger,* 24 Apr. 1985. The last installment of the raise, due in the 1987–88 school year and totaling $1,000, was tied to a classroom evaluation of teachers. Frequently, but erroneously, the pay bill has been referred to as a merit-pay plan.

75. Ibid., 24, 26 Apr. 1985.

76. *Mississippi Code, 1972, Annotated,* sec. 37-3-2, p. 1.

77. Department of Education, *Five-Year Plan, 1986–1990,* III-32.

78. *Meridian Star,* 2 Sept. 1984.

79. Department of Education, *Five-Year Plan, 1986–1990,* III-32.

80. Mississippi State Department of Education, "Teacher and Ad-

ministrator Education, Certification and Development" (Jackson: State Department of Education, July 1986), 4–5. One-year provisional status applies not only to recent college graduates entering the profession for the first time but also to those career teachers and administrators holding regular or standard certificates who were employed in Mississippi since the enactment of the Education Reform Act.

81. Ibid., 7, 16.

82. Mississippi State Department of Education, "Mississippi Teacher Assessment Instruments: Questions and Answers" (Jackson: State Department of Education, July 1987), iii–v; and Mississippi State Department of Education, "Personnel Appraisal Requirements, 1987, 1988 School Year, Memorandum" (Jackson: State Department of Education, 15 Sept. 1987).

83. Mississippi State Department of Education, "Preparing a Comprehensive Staff Development Plan: A Technical Guide" (Jackson: State Department of Education, n.d.), 1.

84. Ibid., 6; and Mississippi State Department of Education, "Staff Development: Questions and Answers for Teachers and Administrators" (Jackson: State Department of Education, Dec. 1985), 12.

85. Mississippi State Department of Education, "Staff Development Reporting" (Memorandum, 4 May 1988); and Department of Education, "Staff Development: Questions and Answers," 12.

86. Mississippi State Department of Education, "The Requirements of the Commission on School Accreditation: Policies, Procedures, and Standards," *Bulletin 171*, 10th ed. (Jackson: State Department of Education, July 1987), xi.

87. Ibid.

88. Ibid.

89. Ibid.

90. *Tupelo Daily Journal*, 8 Aug. 1984.

91. Report of the Task Force for Excellence, *An Opportunity for Excellence: The Mississippi Education Reform Act of 1982* (Meridian: Phil Hardin Foundation, 1983), 35.

92. *Mississippi Code, 1972, Annotated,* sec. 37-17-6, p. 1.

93. Ibid., sec. 37-17-6, p. 4.

94. Department of Education, "The Requirements of the Commission on School Accreditation," 6–9.

95. Department of Education, *Five-Year Plan, 1986–1990,* II-8.

96. *Jackson Clarion-Ledger,* 23 Nov. 1982.

97. Brownlee, "Applying a New Federalism," 1.

98. *Meridian Star,* 4 Sept. 1983.

99. State Legislature, "House Bill No. 4." sec. 26, p. 2.

100. Task Force for Excellence, *Opportunity for Excellence,* 13.

101. *Jackson Clarion-Ledger,* 21 Oct. 1984; and *Neshoba* (Philadelphia, Miss.) *Democrat,* 4 July 1984.

102. *Jackson Clarion-Ledger,* 21 Nov. 1983.

103. Thomas Saterfiel, interview with authors, Jackson, Miss., 27 Jan. 1989. Dr. Saterfiel also pointed out that, while four years ago 100 school districts did not offer a foreign language, only 29 do not provide such an offering today.

Educational Reform in Alabama

1. Charles E. Silberman, *Crisis in the Classroom* (New York: Vintage Books, 1970), vii.

2. Richard J. Altenbaugh, "Teachers, Their World, and Their Work: A Review of the Idea of 'Professional Excellence' in School Reform Reports," in *The New Servants of Power: A Critique of the 1980s School Reform Movement,* ed. Christine M. Shea, Ernest Kahane, and Peter Sola (New York: Greenwood Press, 1989), 167–75.

3. Lawrence Cremin, *The Transformation of the School: Progressivism in American Education, 1876–1957* (New York: Vintage Books, 1964).

4. William B. Lauderdale, "Current Evaluations of Alabama Teachers: An Historical Perspective" (Paper presented at the annual meeting of the National Council on Measurement in Education, 21 Apr. 1987).

5. Ibid., 6.

6. Truman M. Pierce, "Teacher Education: Past, Present, and Future," *Professional Educator* 1 (Spring 1978):1–22.

7. *Professional Educator* 1 (Spring 1978).

8. National Commission on Excellence in Education, *A Nation at Risk: The Imperative for Educational Reform* (Washington, D.C.: U.S. Government Printing Office, 1983), 5.

9. Henry A. Giroux, "Citizenship, Public Philosophy, and the Struggle for Democracy," *Educational Theory* 37 (Spring 1987):112.

10. *Montgomery Advertiser,* 10 Aug. 1984.

11. *A Nation at Risk,* 18–22.

12. Ibid., 22–23.

13. Holmes Group, *Tomorrow's Teachers* (East Lansing, Mich.: Holmes Group, Apr. 1986), 26–27.

14. Wayne Teague, "Teacher Education and Professional Develop-

ment in Alabama from the Viewpoint of the State Superintendent," *Professional Educator* 1 (Spring 1978):iii.

15. Ibid.

16. Hans-George Gadamer, *Reason in the Age of Science* (Cambridge: MIT Press, 1981), esp. 69–169; and Robert Hollinger, ed., *Hermeneutics and Praxis* (South Bend: University of Notre Dame Press, 1985).

17. John Dewey, *The Sources of a Science of Education* (New York: Liveright, 1929), 14–15.

18. William B. Lauderdale, *Educational Reform: The Forgotten Half* (Bloomington, Ind.: Phi Delta Kappa Educational Foundation, 1987), 30.

19. Ibid.

The Illusion of Reform in Georgia

1. Governor's Education Review Commission, *Priority for a Quality Basic Education,* 12 Nov. 1984, 2.

2. Ibid., 19.

3. Ibid., 3.

4. Jane O. Hansen, "QBE Funds Often Used to Cut Taxes," *Atlanta Journal and Constitution,* 4 Jan. 1987.

5. Georgia General Assembly, Committee of Conference Substitute to SB 82 (n.d.), 6.

6. Arthur E. Wise, *Legislated Learning: The Bureaucratization of the American Classroom* (Berkeley and Los Angeles: University of California Press, 1979).

7. Reports of students cheating on the tests and of primary-age youngsters becoming physically ill as test time grew near followed the implementation of the QBE testing provisions; see Monte Plott, "House Panel Tells of Cheating Reports on Basic School Tests," *Atlanta Constitution,* 28 Feb. 1986; and Susan Lacetti, "Students Grow Weary of Testing," *Atlanta Journal and Constitution,* 11 May 1986.

8. Wayne J. Urban, with Don Martin and George Overholt, *Accountability in American Education: A Critique* (Princeton: Princeton Book Co., 1976), chap. 3.

9. Michael W. Apple, *Teachers and Texts* (New York: Routledge, 1988).

10. Raymond E. Callahan, *Education and the Cult of Efficiency: A Study of the Social Forces that Have Shaped the Administration of the Public Schools* (Chicago: University of Chicago Press, 1962); and

Wayne J. Urban, "The Past and the Present in Educational Innovation: Scientific Management and Competency Based Education," *Foundational Studies* 6 (Spring-Summer 1977):5–17.

11. Committee of Conference Substitute to SB 82, 156.

12. Wayne J. Urban, "Merit Pay and Organized Teachers in the USA," in *The Politics of Teacher Unionism,* ed. Martin Lawn (London: Croom Helm, 1985).

13. Ibid.

Imagining Sisyphus Happy with Reformers

1. Henry Levin, "A Taxonomy of Educational Reforms for Changes in the Nature of Work," in *The Limits of Educational Reform,* ed. Martin Carnoy and Henry Levin (New York: David McKay, 1976).

2. Paul Ricoeur, *Freud and Philosophy,* trans. Denis Savage (New Haven: Yale University Press, 1970), 27.

3. Martin Heidegger, *Kant and the Problem of Metaphysics,* trans. J. S. Churchill (Bloomington: Indiana University Press, 1962).

4. Gaston Bachelard, *Psychoanalysis of Fire,* trans. Alan Ross (Boston: Beacon Press, 1968); and Edward Casey, *Imagining* (Bloomington: Indiana University Press, 1976).

5. Martin Heidegger, *Being and Time,* trans. J. Macquarrie and E. Robinson (New York: Harper and Row, 1962); and Gaston Bachelard, *The Poetics of Space,* trans. Maria Jolas (Boston: Beacon Press, 1969).

6. David E. Denton, "Between Concepts and Experience: Bachelard and Freud," published as "Entre les concepts et l'experience: Bachelard et Freud," *Cahiers Internationaux de Symbolisme,* trans. Cecil Rees-de Jaegher, 53-54-55 (1986):125–39.

7. Gaston Bachelard, *The Poetics of Reverie,* trans. Daniel Russell (Boston: Beacon Press, 1971).

8. Albert Camus, *The Myth of Sisyphus,* trans. Justin O'Brien (New York: Vintage Books, 1959).

9. Ibid., 91.

10. David E. Denton, "Images, Plausibility and Truth," *Futures Research Quarterly* 2 (Summer 1986):53–62.

The Future of the Public School

1. Onalee McGraw, *Family Choice in Education: The New Imperative* (Washington, D.C.: Heritage Foundation, 1978), 22.

2. John Stuart Mill, *Essential Works of John Stuart Mill,* ed. Max

Lerner (New York: Bantam Books, 1961), 351. (Emphasis added.)

3. Elliott Eisner, *The Educational Imagination: On the Design and Evaluation of School Programs* (New York: Macmillan, 1985), 2.

4. Stephen Arons, "The Separation of School and State: *Pierce* Reconsidered," *Harvard Educational Review* 46, no. 1 (Feb. 1976):77.

5. Ibid., 77–102.

6. McGraw, *Family Choice,* 40.

7. Michael Littleford, "Censorship, Academic Freedom, and the Public School Teacher" (Paper presented at "A Summit Conference on Quality Education in Alabama," sponsored by the Alabama Education Association and the Alabama Association of Colleges of Teacher Education, Montgomery, Ala., 10–11 Dec. 1982), 16.

8. Robert Church, *Education in the United States* (New York: Free Press, 1976), 58–80.

9. David Tyack, *The One Best System* (Cambridge: Harvard University Press, 1974), 141.

Bibliography

Books

Akin, Edward N. *Mississippi, An Illustrated History*. Northridge, Calif.: Windsor Publications, 1987.

Alexander, Kern, and Kenneth Forbis Jordan. *Legal Aspects of Educational Choice: Compulsory Attendance and Student Assignment*. Topeka: National Organization on Legal Problems of Education, 1973.

Altbach, P. G., G. P. Kelly, and L. Weis, eds. *Excellence in Education: Perspectives on Policy and Practice*. Buffalo: Prometheus Books, 1985.

Anderson, R. C., and D. P. Ausubel, eds. *Readings in the Psychology of Cognition*. New York: Holt, Rinehart and Winston, 1965.

Apple, Michael W. *Teachers and Texts*. New York: Routledge, 1988.

Bachelard, Gaston. *The Poetics of Reverie*. Translated by Daniel Russell. Boston: Beacon Press, 1971.

——. *The Poetics of Space*. Translated by Maria Jolas. Boston: Beacon Press, 1969.

——. *Psychoanalysis of Fire*. Translated by Alan Ross. Boston: Beacon Press, 1968.

Bagley, William C. *Classroom Management: Its Principles and Technique*. New York: Macmillan, 1908.

Baldridge, J. V., and T. Deal, eds. *The Dynamics of Organizational Change in Education*. Berkeley, Calif.: McCutchan, 1983.

Boaz, D., ed. *Left, Right and Babyboom: America's New Politics*. Washington, D.C.: CATO Institute, 1986.

Booz-Allen & Hamilton Report, Summary of State-Wide Education Study, Phase I, State of Mississippi. Jackson: State of Mississippi, 1967.

Boyd, William Lowe, and D. Smart, eds. *Educational Policy in Australia and America: Comparative Perspectives*. New York: Falmer Press, 1987.

Boyer, Ernest L. *Teacher Involvement in Decisionmaking: A State-by-State Profile*. Washington, D.C.: Carnegie Foundation for the Advancement of Teaching, Sept. 1988.

Brandwein, Paul. *Memorandum: On Renewing Schooling and Education.* New York: Harcourt Brace Jovanovich, 1981.

Callahan, Raymond E. *Education and the Cult of Efficiency: A Study of the Social Forces that Have Shaped the Administration of the Public Schools.* Chicago: University of Chicago Press, 1962.

Camus, Albert. *The Myth of Sisyphus.* Translated by Justin O'Brien. New York: Vintage Books, 1959.

Carnegie Commission on Education and the Economy. *Report of the Task Force on Teaching as a Profession.* Princeton, N.J.: Carnegie Foundation for the Advancement of Teaching, 1986.

Carnoy, Martin, and Henry Levin. *The Limits of Educational Reform.* New York: David McKay, 1976.

Casey, Edward. *Imagining.* Bloomington: Indiana University Press, 1976.

Church, Robert. *Education in the United States.* New York: Free Press, 1976.

A Compilation of the Constitutional Provisions and Legislative Acts Pertaining to the Common Schools in the State of Mississippi. Jackson: Power and Barksdale, 1876.

Corcoran, T., and B. Wilson. *The Search for Successful Secondary Schools: The First Three Years of the Secondary School Recognition Program.* Philadelphia: Research for Better Schools, Oct. 1986.

Cremin, Lawrence. *The Transformation of the School: Progressivism in American Education, 1876–1957.* New York: Vintage Books, 1964.

Dewey, John. *The Sources of a Science of Education.* New York: Liveright, 1929.

Drucker, Peter F. *The Practice of Management.* New York: Harper and Brothers, 1954.

Eisner, Elliot W. *The Educational Imagination: On the Design and Evaluation of School Programs.* New York: Macmillan, 1985.

Gadamer, Hans-George. *Reason in the Age of Science,* Cambridge: MIT Press, 1981.

Gill, Gerald R. *Meanness Mania: The Changed Mood.* Washington, D.C.: Howard University Press, 1980.

Gregory, T. B., and G. R. Smith. *High Schools as Communities: The Small School Reconsidered.* Bloomington, Ind.: Phi Delta Kappa Educational Foundation, 1987.

Guthrie, James W., ed. *School Finance Policies and Practices—The 1980s: A Decade of Conflict.* Cambridge, Mass.: Ballinger, 1980.

Hand, William H. *The Need of Compulsory Education in the South.* Washington, D.C.: United States Bureau of Education, Bulletin, No. 2, 1914.

Heidegger, Martin. *Being and Time.* Translated by J. Macquarrie and E. Robinson. New York: Harper and Row, 1962.

————. *Kant and the Problem of Metaphysics.* Translated by J. S. Churchill. Bloomington: Indiana University Press, 1962.

Hollinger, Robert, ed. *Hermeneutics and Praxis.* South Bend: University of Notre Dame Press, 1985.

Holmes Group. *Tomorrow's Teachers.* East Lansing, Mich.: Holmes Group, 1986.

Holmes, William F. *The White Chief: James Kimble Vardaman.* Baton Rouge: Louisiana State University Press, 1970.

Hutchins, Robert, ed. *The Great Books of the Western World,* vol. 12. Chicago: Encyclopedia Britannica, 1952.

Kirst, M. W. *Who Controls Our Schools? American Values in Conflict.* Stanford: Stanford Alumni Association, 1984.

Lauderdale, William B. *Educational Reform: The Forgotten Half.* Bloomington, Ind.: Phi Delta Kappa Educational Foundation, 1987.

Lawn, Martin, ed. *The Politics of Teacher Unionism.* London: Croom Helm, 1985.

Lightfoot, S. L. *The Good High School: Portraits of Character and Culture.* New York: Basic Books, 1983.

McGraw, Onalee. *Family Choice in Education: The New Imperative.* Washington, D.C.: Heritage Foundation, 1978.

Mann, D., ed. *Making Change Happen?* New York: Teachers College Press, 1978.

Mayes, Edward. *History of Education in Mississippi.* Washington, D.C.: United States Bureau of Education, 1899.

Mill, John Stuart. *Essential Works of John Stuart Mill.* Edited by Max Lerner. New York: Bantam Books, 1961.

Mississippi State Department of Education. *Biennial Report and Recommendations of the State Superintendent, 1915–16.* Jackson: State Department of Education, 1916.

Mississippi State Department of Education. *Biennial Report and Recommendations of the State Superintendent, 1920–21.* Jackson: State Department of Education, 1921.

Mississippi State Department of Education. *Biennial Report, 1924–25.* Jackson: State Department of Education, 1925.

Mississippi State Department of Education. *Biennial Report, 1965–67.* Jackson: State Department of Education, 1967.

Mississippi State Department of Education. *A Compilation of the School Laws of Mississippi.* Jackson: State of Mississippi, Department of Education, 1958.

Mississippi State Department of Education. *Five-Year Plan for Educational Improvement, Support Document, 1986–1990.* Jackson: State Department of Education, 1986.

Mississippi State Department of Education. *Mississippi Statewide Testing: Pupil Performance, 1988.* Jackson: State Department of Education, 1988.

Murphy, Sara, ed. *Fulfilling the Promise of Reform: Arkansas Reform Study, 1985–88.* Little Rock: Winthrop Rockefeller Foundation, Dec. 1988.

National Commission for Excellence in Teacher Education. *A Call for Change in Teacher Education.* Washington, D.C.: American Association of Colleges for Teacher Education, 1985.

National Commission on Excellence in Education. *A Nation at Risk: The Imperative for Educational Reform.* Washington, D.C.: U.S. Government Printing Office, 1983.

Noble, Stuart G. *Forty Years of the Public Schools in Mississippi.* 1918. Reprint. New York: AMS Press, 1972.

Pearson, Jim B., and Edgar Fuller. *Education in the States: Historical Development and Outlook.* Washington, D.C.: National Education Association of the United States, 1969.

Peters, T. J., and R. H. Waterman, Jr. *In Search of Excellence: Lessons from America's Best-Run Companies.* New York: Harper and Row, 1982.

Peterson, Paul E. *City Limits.* Chicago: University of Chicago Press, 1981.

————. *The Politics of School Reform, 1870–1940.* Chicago: University of Chicago Press, 1985.

Public Education Study Committee. *A Study of Critical Issues in Mississippi's Public Schools with Recommendations and Legislative Proposals for Improving the Public Educational System in the State (Summary Report).* Jackson: State of Mississippi, 1973.

Report of the Task Force for Excellence. *An Opportunity for Excellence: The Mississippi Education Reform Act of 1982.* Meridian: Phil Hardin Foundation, 1983.

Ricoeur, Paul. *Freud and Philosophy.* Translated by Denis Savage. New Haven: Yale University Press, 1970.

Rutter, Michael, Barbara Maughan, Peter Mortimore, and Janet Ouston, with Alan Smith. *Fifteen Thousand Hours: Secondary*

Schools and Their Effects on Children. Cambridge: Harvard University Press, 1979.

Sarason, S. B. *The Culture of the School and the Problem of Chance*. 2d ed. Boston: Allyn and Bacon, 1982.

Schein, E. H. *Organizational Psychology*. Englewood Cliffs, N.J.: Prentice-Hall, 1965.

Shea, Christine M., Ernest Kahane, and Peter Sola, eds. *The New Servants of Power: A Critique of the 1980s School Reform Movement*. New York: Greenwood Press, 1989.

Shulman, Lee S., and G. Sykes, eds. *Handbook of Teaching and Policy*. New York: Longman, 1983.

Silberman, Charles E. *Crisis in the Classroom*. New York: Vintage Books, 1970.

Skates, John Ray. *Mississippi, A Bicentennial History*. New York: Norton Press, 1979.

Tyack, David. *The One Best System*. Cambridge: Harvard University Press, 1974.

Tye, Barbara B. *Multiple Realities: A Study of 13 American High Schools*. Lanham, Md.: University Press of America, 1985.

Urban, Wayne J., with Don Martin and George Overholt. *Accountability in American Education: A Critique*. Princeton: Princeton Book Co., 1976.

Wayson, William W. *Up from Excellence: The Impact of the Excellence Movement on Schools*. Bloomington, Ind.: Phi Delta Kappa Educational Foundation, 1986.

Wise, Arthur E. *Legislated Learning: The Bureaucratization of the American Classroom*. Berkeley and Los Angeles: University of California Press, 1979.

Articles and Papers

Arons, Stephen. "The Separation of School and State: *Pierce* Reconsidered." *Harvard Educational Review* 46, no. 1 (Feb. 1976).

Boyd, William Lowe. "Local Influences on Education." In *Encyclopedia of Educational Research*. 5th ed. New York: Macmillan and Free Press, 1982.

Brown, Charles A. "Only School Users Should Pay For Them." *Tuscaloosa News*, 18 Oct. 1987.

Brownlee, Ron. "Applying a New Federalism Solution to the Problem of Educational Deprivation: An Assessment of the Implementation of Mississippi's 1982 Education Reform Act." Mississippi State

University Library, Special Collections, n.d.

Clark, B. R. "The High School and the University: What Went Wrong in America, Part I." *Phi Delta Kappan* 66 (Feb. 1985).

———. "The High School and the University: What Went Wrong in America, Part II." *Phi Delta Kappan* 66 (March 1985).

Clark, D. L., and T. A. Astuto. "The Significance and Permanence of Changes in Federal Education Policy." *Educational Researcher* 15, no. 8 (1986).

Clinton, Bill. "Who Will Manage the Schools?" *Phi Delta Kappan* 68 (Nov. 1986).

———. "We've Made Progress in Education, but the Job Isn't Over." *Arkansas Gazette,* 13 Dec. 1987.

Columbus Commercial Dispatch, 1 Mar. 1982, 7 April 1982, 5 Sept. 1984.

Cornbleth, Catherine. "Knowledge in Curriculum and Teacher Education." *Social Education* 51 (1987).

Denton, David E. "Between Concepts and Experience: Bachelard and Freud." Published as "Entre les concepts et l'experience: Bachelard et Freud." *Cahiers Internationaux de Symbolisme.* Translated by Cecil Rees-de Jaegher, 53-54-55 (1986).

———. "Images, Plausibility and Truth." *Futures Research Quarterly* 2 (Summer 1986).

DeVitis, Joseph L. "State Education Reforms Lower Morale." *Jackson* (Tennessee) *Sun,* 15 Feb. 1987.

Emery, F. E., and E. L. Trist. "The Causal Texture of Organizational Environments." *Human Relations* 18 (1965).

Evangelauf, J. "School-Reform Movement Said to Be Moving from Capitols to Classrooms." *Chronicle of Higher Education,* 7 May 1986.

Florida School Laws, 1985 Edition.

Georgia General Assembly. Committee of Conference Substitute to SB 82, n.d.

Giroux, Henry A. "Citizenship, Public Philosophy, and the Struggle for Democracy." *Educational Theory* 37 (Spring 1987).

The Governor's Education Review Commission. *Priority for a Quality Basic Education,* 12 Nov. 1984.

Guthrie, James W. "School-Based Management: The Next Needed Education Reform." *Phi Delta Kappan* 68 (Dec. 1986).

Hansen, Jane O. "QBE Funds Often Used to Cut Taxes." *Atlanta Journal and Constitution,* 4 Jan. 1987.

Harris, Marshall A. "Memorandum to Members of the Florida Education Council," Tallahassee: Florida Department of Education, 20 June 1984.

Hawley, Willis D. "Toward a Comprehensive Strategy for Addressing the Teacher Shortage." *Phi Delta Kappan* 67 (June 1986).

Jackson Clarion-Ledger, 24 Oct. 1982, 23 Nov. 1982, 28 Nov. 1982, 7 Dec. 1982, 3 Jan. 1983, 18 Nov. 1983, 21 Nov. 1983, 28 Apr. 1984, 21 Oct. 1984, 20 Nov. 1984, 24 Apr. 1985, 5 May 1985, 14 July 1985.

Johnson, S. M. "Incentives for Teachers: What Motivates, What Matters." *Educational Administration Quarterly* 22, no. 3 (1986).

Jung, R. K., and M. W. Kirst. "Beyond Mutual Adaptation, Into the Bully Pulpit: Recent Research on the Federal Role in Education." *Educational Administration Quarterly* 22, no. 3 (1986).

Kirst, M. W. "Curricular Leadership at the State Level: What Is the New Focus?" *NASSP Bulletin* (Apr. 1987).

Lacetti, Susan. "Students Grow Weary of Testing." *Atlanta Journal and Constitution,* 11 May 1986.

Lauderdale, William B. "Current Evaluations of Alabama Teachers: An Historical Perspective." Paper presented at the annual meeting of the National Council on Measurement in Education, 21 Apr. 1987.

Levary, M. "Few Teachers Back Career Ladder, Survey Says." *Knoxville News-Sentinel,* 25 Feb. 1986.

Littleford, Michael. "Censorship, Academic Freedom, and the Public School Teacher." Paper presented at "A Summit Conference on Quality Education in Alabama," sponsored by the Alabama Education Association and the Alabama Association of Colleges of Teacher Education, Montgomery, Ala., 10–11 Dec. 1982.

McCain, William D. "Education in Mississippi in 1860." *Journal of Mississippi History* 22 (Jan.–Oct. 1960).

McNeil, L. M. "Exit, Voice and Community: Magnet Teachers' Responses to Standardization." Paper presented at American Educational Research Association annual meeting, San Francisco, Apr. 1986.

Malen, B., and A. W. Hart, "Career Ladder Reform: A Multi-level Analysis of Initial Efforts. *Educational Evaluation and Policy Analysis* 9, no. 1 (1987).

March, J. G., and J. P. Olsen. "Organizing Political Life: What Administrative Reorganization Tells Us about Government." *American Political Science Review* 22 (June 1983).

Memphis Commercial Appeal, 1 Aug. 1979, 13 Nov. 1982, 4 Dec. 1982.

Meridian Star, 4 Sept. 1983, 2 Sept. 1984.

Mississippi Code, 1972, Annotated Cumulative Supplement.

"The Mississippi Reform Act Five Years Later, A Report to the People of Mississippi from Dr. Richard A. Boyd, State Superintendent of Education." Jackson: State Department of Education, 1987.

Mississippi State Department of Education. *Five-Year Plan, 1986–1990.*

Mississippi State Department of Education. "Mississippi School District Profile, 1987–88, Lowndes County School District." Jackson: State Department of Education, 1988.

Mississippi State Department of Education. "Mississippi Teacher Assessment Instruments: Questions and Answers." Jackson: State Department of Education, July 1987.

Mississippi State Department of Education. "1985–1986 School Year Report on BSAP, FLE, ACT for Mississippi." Jackson: State Department of Education, n.d.

Mississippi State Department of Education. "Preparing a Comprehensive Staff Development Plan: A Technical Guide." Jackson: State Department of Education, n.d.

Mississippi State Department of Education. "The Requirements of the Commission on School Accreditation: Policies, Procedures, and Standards." *Bulletin 171.* 10th ed. Jackson: State Department of Education, July 1987.

Mississippi State Department of Education. "School Dropouts by Reason, 1987–1988." Jackson: State Department of Education, n.d.

Mississippi State Department of Education. "Staff Development: Questions and Answers for Teachers and Administrators." Jackson: State Department of Education, Dec. 1985.

Mississippi State Department of Education. "Staff Development Reporting." Memorandum, 4 May 1988.

Mississippi State Department of Education. "Teacher and Administrator Education, Certification and Development." Jackson: State Department of Education, July 1986.

Mississippi State Legislature. "House Bill No. 4," sec. 12.

Montgomery Advertiser, 10 Aug. 1984.

Neshoba Democrat (Philadelphia, Miss.), 4 July 1984.

Odden, Allan. "Education Finance 1985: A Rising Tide or Steady Fiscal State?" *Educational Evaluation and Policy Analysis* 7 no. 4 (1985).

———. "When Votes and Dollars Mingle: A First Analysis of State Reforms." *Politics of Education Bulletin* 13, no. 2 (1986).

Odden, Allan, and B. Anderson. "How Successful State Education Improvement Programs Work." *Phi Delta Kappan* 67 (Apr. 1986).

Passow, A. Harry. "Tackling the Reform Reports of the 1980s." *Phi Delta Kappan* 65 (June 1984).

Person, William A., and Robert L. Jenkins. "A Documentary and Interpretive History of Compulsory School Attendance Laws in Mississippi: A Preliminary Report." Paper presented at the 1984 annual conference of the Southeastern Regional Association of Teacher Educators, Williamsburg, Va., Nov. 1984.

"Personnel Appraisal Requirements, 1987, 1988 School Year, Memorandum." Jackson: State Department of Education, 15 Sept. 1987.

Peterson, K. D., J. Murphy, and P. Hallinger. "Superintendents' Perceptions of the Control and Coordination of the Technical Core in Effective School Districts." *Educational Administration Quarterly* 23, no. 1 (1987).

Peterson, Paul E. "Did the Education Commissions Say Anything?" Brookings Review 2 (1983).

———. "Economic and Political Trends Affecting Education." Paper presented at the Brookings Institution, Washington, D.C., n.d.

Pierce, Truman M. "Teacher Education: Past, Present, and Future." *Professional Educator* 1 (Spring 1978).

Plank, D. "The Ayes of Texas: Rhetoric, Reality, and School Reform." *Politics of Education Bulletin* 13, no. 2 (1986).

Plott, Monte. "House Panel Tells of Cheating Reports on Basic School Tests." *Atlanta Constitution*, 28 Feb. 1986.

Popkewitz, Thomas S. "Organization and Power: Teacher Education Reforms." *Social Education* 51 (1987).

Quie, Albert H. "More 'Choice' Is Key to Public-School Reform." *Education Week,* 20 May 1987.

Shanker, Albert. "The First Real Crisis." In *Handbook of Teaching and Policy.* Edited by L. S. Shulman and G. Sykes. New York: Longman, 1983.

Shulman, Lee S. "Knowledge and Teaching: Foundations of the New Reform." *Harvard Educational Review* 57 (Feb. 1987).

Silver, Paula F. "Review of *Organizational Environments: Ritual and Rationality.*" *Educational Administration Quarterly* 22, no. 2 (1986).

Standards for Accreditation: Arkansas Public Schools. State Board of Education, 19 Feb. 1984.

Starkville Daily News, 25 Oct. 1982, 4 May 1985.

Sumners, Mary F. "Education in Ante-bellum Tishomingo County." *Journal of Mississippi History* 20 (Jan.–Oct. 1958).

Task Force for Excellence. *An Opportunity for Excellence.*

"Teacher Evaluations Need to Be Custom Made." *Phi Delta Kappan* 68 (Jan. 1987).

"Teachers Found Skeptical about Impact of Reforms." *Education Week,* 19 Nov. 1986.

Teague, Wayne. "Teacher Education and Professional Development in Alabama from the Viewpoint of the State Superintendent." *Professional Educator* 1 (Spring 1978).

Timar, T. B., and D. L. Kirp, "Education Reform in the 1980s: Lessons from the States." *Phi Delta Kappan* 70 (Mar. 1989).

Tupelo Daily Journal, 8 Aug. 1984.

Tye, Barbara B. "The Deep Structure of Schooling." *Phi Delta Kappan* 69 (Dec. 1987).

Tyler, Ralph W. "Education Reforms." *Phi Delta Kappan* 69 (Dec. 1987).

Urban, Wayne J. "The Past and the Present in Educational Innovation: Scientific Management and Competency Based Education." *Foundational Studies* 6 (Spring-Summer 1977).

Weatherley, R., and M. Lipsky. "Street-Level Bureaucrats and Institutional Innovation: Implementing Special-Education Reform." *Harvard Educational Review* 47, no. 2 (May 1977).

Winter, William. "Speech to the Mississippi Economic Council, 13 May 1981." Governor's Papers. Record Group 27, Box 1314, Mississippi Department of Archives and History, Jackson.

Wirt, Fred M. "National Australia-United States Education: A Commentary." In *Educational Policy in Australia and America: Comparative Perspectives.* Edited by William Lowe Boyd and D. Smart. New York: Falmer Press, 1987.

Wise, Arthur E. "Legislated Learning Revisited." *Phi Delta Kappan* 69 (Jan. 1988).

Contributors

William Lowe Boyd is Professor of Education at Pennsylvania State University, where he has taught since 1980. He is the co-editor of six books, including *Educational Policy in Australia and America, The Politics of Excellence and Choice in Education,* and *Private Schools and Public Policy.*

David E. Denton is Professor and Director of Graduate Studies in the Department of Educational Policy Studies and Evaluation at the University of Kentucky. He has a distinguished publication record, with over eighty articles and nine books to his credit, including *The Philosophy of Albert Camus, Existential Reflections on Teaching,* and *Gaia's Drum: Ancient Voices and Our Children's Future.*

Joseph L. DeVitis has recently moved from the University of Tennessee at Martin to the State University of New York at Binghamton, where he is Professor of Education and Human Development and Program Coordinator, Master of Arts in Social Sciences. He has written widely on morality, culture and reform. His books include *Theories of Moral Development* and *Helping and Intervention: Comparative Perspectives on the Impossible Professions* (written with John Martin Rich).

Robert L. Jenkins is Assistant Professor of History at Mississippi State University. He has written on questions of economics and geography in Africa and on the history of black higher education in Mississippi. His work has been published in *Cameroon and Chad at the Crossroads: A Study in Contrast, Encyclopedia of Southern Culture,* and *Journal of Mississippi History.*

Robert W. Johns is Associate Professor in the Department of Teacher Education at the University of Arkansas at Little Rock. He has published in such journals as *Theory and Research in Social Education, Art Education,* and *Educational Studies,* principally in the areas of history, global education, politics, and art education.

C. J. B. Macmillan is Professor of Philosophy of Education at Florida State University and served as President of The Philosophy of Education Society in 1984. He has published widely in such journals as *Educational Theory, Teachers College Record,* and *Educational Forum.* Also, along with Jim Garrison, he has written *A Logical Theory of Teaching.*

Kenneth D. McCracken is Professor of Education at the University of Tennessee at Martin, where he has taught since 1962. His writing has focused on social studies and issues pertaining to educational aims, and his work has been published in *Educational Catalyst, Educational Studies,* and *Contemporary Education.*

William A. Person is Associate Professor of Curriculum and Instruction at Mississippi State University. His work has been published in *Resources in Education, FOCUS,* and *Educational and Psychological Research,* on such topics as the effectiveness of research applications, perceptions of achievement testing, and student teachers' classroom performance.

Charles F. Rudder is Assistant Professor of History and Philosophy of Education at The University of Alabama. He has written on such topics as pragmatism, philosophy of science, ethics, and educational policy, with publications in *Critical Issues in Philosophy of Education* and *Educational Theory.*

Wayne J. Urban is Research Professor of Educational Foundations and Professor of History at Georgia State University. Well known as an author and editor of *Educational Studies,* his books include *Why Teachers Organized, Black Scholar: Horace Mann Bond, 1904–1972* and *Accountability in American Education: A Critique* (written with Don Martin and George Overholt).

David J. Vold is Professor and Chair of the Program of History, Philosophy and Sociology of Education at The University of Alabama. His work on issues of religion, morality, democracy, and teacher testing has appeared in such journals as *Educational Theory, Educational Studies* and *Educational Measurement: Issues and Practice.* He has recently completed *A Student's Guide to Philosophy of Education.*

Index